SOME PROOFS OF THE EXTERNAL WORLD :

INTERPRETATIONS AND CRITICISMS

SOME PROOFS OF THE EXTERNAL WORLD :

Interpretations And Criticisms

By

Rina Mukhopadhyay

MAHA BODHI BOOK AGENCY
4A, Bankim Chatterjee Street, College Square
Kolkata - 700 073, (India)
2017

SOME PROOFS OF THE EXTERNAL WORLD : INTERPRETATIONS AND CRITICISMS

by

RINA MUKHOPADHYAY

First Published : 2017

Published by :
D.L.S. Jayawardana
MAHA BODHI BOOK AGENCY
4A, Bankim Chatterjee Street, College Square
Kolkata-700 073, (India)
Phone : 9831077368, 9831529452
Email : mahabodhibookagency@hotmail.com

Printed by :
Sagarika Press, Kolkata-700 009

ISBN : 978-93-84721-42-8

Price : ₹ 500/-

Dedicated

To The memory of
my mother

Maya Mukherjee
and of

my elder brother
Goutam Mukherjee,

Whose blessings have always been
a source of inspiration for me

a dictate of nature - , as was pointed out before. Now, the natural belief or teaching that material things produce sensory ideas is not liable to correction by any kind or amount of rational argument. For Descartes, a rationally incorrigible natural teaching is a teaching of God through my nature which is given me by Him[48]. Gilson has simply failed to appreciate the importance of the teaching of nature for Descartes' treatment of the problem of the existence of material things.

In Gilson's second account there is, at one stage of it, the occurrence of the phrase 'this spontaneous and natural *reasoning*'[49]. Neither the expression itself nor (as Stout has observed) the context in which the expression is used makes it clear what precisely Gilson means by it. The adjective 'spontaneous and natural' is strongly suggestive of a natural and spontaneous belief. If now Gilson means by this expression to signify a natural belief, then he is surely guilty of a confusion[50]; for a natural belief is not an act of *reasoning* at all; it is only a belief. This belief, even if it is rationally incorrigible, in the sense of being resistant to rational criticism, does not thereby become an act of *reasoning* itself. So the phrase 'spontaneous and natural *reasoning*' is, to put it mildly, highly disturbing.

A detailed examination of Gilson's interpretation of the Cartesian proof of the external world has been made, and it has been found that the interpretation is unsatisfactory.

2.4 Consideration of an Issue Raised by the Doctrine of the Veracity of God

The doctrine of the veracity of God - on the Cartesian understanding that God exists - does not give rise to any problem if it is formulated by saying that God is not a deceiver or that He does not deceive, but a serious problem arises if it is formulated by saying that God cannot deceive, because the modal 'cannot' appears to signify a kind of limitation or inability which is incompatible with the omnipotence of God. It is interesting to see how Descartes seeks to avoid the problem by choosing to formulate the doctrine usually in the first way, avoiding the second way of formulating it in most cases, and responding to his critics in appropriate and cautious ways.

Jonathan Bennett observes[51] that the doctrine of the veracity of God comes up in more than forty passages in Descartes' writings, and that in the majority of them Descartes expresses his view by saying only that God *does not* deceive, that is, without using the modal 'cannot'.

Even when Descartes is invited by Mersenne to say something stronger, he does not take the bait, but responds by expressing his view in the non-modal way: 'In saying that God does not lie, and is not a deceiver . . . .'[52]

Sometimes, however, Descartes adopts a different strategy in his reply to his critics, namely, the strategy of transferring the inability signified by the modal 'cannot' from God on to man. Thus, when Hobbes says, 'Descartes should consider the proposition "God can in no case deceive us" and see whether it is universally true', Descartes in his reply begins by recasting 'God can in no case deceive us' as 'We can in no case be deceived'[53]. His full reply to Hobbes does not matter; what is of interest at present is - as Bennett puts it - 'his switch of propositions, removing the modal operator from God's deceiving on to our being deceived'[54] - that is, his transferring of the inability signified by 'cannot' from God on to ourselves.

Descartes sometimes formulates his doctrine in terms of impossibility. Thus in *Meditation IV he* says: 'it is impossible for him [Him] ever to deceive me, ...'[55]. The question is how the word 'impossible' in such contexts is to be interpreted. Bennett suggests that the impossibility here is to be interpreted not as signifying an inability or limitation on the part of God, but as rather signifying the impossibility of a certain proposition[56]. The impossibility of a proposition in its turn means its unthinkability by us, that is, its being not thinkable without a contradiction by us. Thus, 'It is impossible for God ever to deceive me' comes to 'The proposition that God ever deceives me is impossible, in the defined sense of being not consistently thinkable by me'. The point is that the matter is to be handled *de dicto,* in terms of the impossibility of a proposition, rather than *de re,* in terms of an inability of God.

Bennett supports the interpretation of 'It is impossible for God ever to deceive me' in terms of the impossibility, or self-contradictoriness, of a proposition by citing some passages from Descartes' work. It will suffice here to quote only two of them, and one of them only in part :

(1) It is a complete contradiction to suppose that he [i.e.God] might deceive me . . . .

[cited from *The Principles of Philosophy.*][57]

(2) It is quite inconsistent with the nature of God that he [He] should be a deceiver.

[cited again from the same work.][58]

Just once in the *Meditations* - in *Meditation III* - Descartes ascribes to God an inability to deceive, observing: 'whence it is sufficiently manifest that he [God] cannot be a deceiver, since . . . . all fraud and deception spring from some defect.'[59] Perhaps even here one may be tempted to think that Descartes' observation to the effect that God cannot be a deceiver allows of being interpreted as an observation having the meaning that 'God is a deceiver' is an impossible (i.e. inconsistent) proposition. But one cannot be sure about this; at least Bennett is not[60]. The reason may be that the context is one in which the *nature* of God is under consideration, and that therefore Descartes' observation here is better construed *de re* than *de dicto.* But if so, then it must be acknowledged that there is here a departure on Descartes' part from his general practice (on Bennett's interpretation) of handling the matter rather *de dicto* than *de re.*

Another misfitting turn of phrase occurs in Descartes' *Principles of Philosophy,* Part II, section 20. He there says that even if God had not made some portion of matter divisible by any creature, He *could not* thereby take away His own power of dividing it. Bennett here observes: 'This, taken strictly, credits God with an incapacity'[61]. He, however, explains this by saying: 'it is a uniquely special one - the inability to give oneself an inability'[62].

So far about the interpretative aspect of an issue raised by the doctrine of the veracity of God.

In the last chapter and the present one Descartes' proof of the existence of external, material, things has been explained in all its important aspects. A critical examination of this proof remains to be undertaken. The next chapter is devoted to that.

NOTES

1 For the expression 'dictate of nature', see Veitch's translation: Everyman's Library edition, p. 134; Mentor Book *(Ten Great Works of Philosophy,* ed. R. P. Wolff), 1969, p. 166.

2 *Meditation VI;* Everyman, pp. 134-135; Mentor, p. 166.

3 A. K. Stout, 'Descartes' Proof of the Existence of Matter', *Philosophy,* vol. I, 1961, p. 194.

4 *Ibidem.*

5 The importance of the role of rationally incorrigible teachings of nature in the Cartesian epistemology, generally overlooked as it is by scholars, is nevertheless recognized and highlighted by two notable commentators: A. K. Stout and Norman Kemp Smith. See Stout's article referred in note 3 above, pp. 191 - 207, and Kemp Smith, *New Studies in the Philosophy of Descartes,* Macmillan, London, 1952, pp. 247 - 258 and 286 -293.

6 See below, 2.3.2.4 of the present work.

7 *Meditation VI:* Everyman, p. 134; Mentor, p. 166.

8 Everyman, pp. 134-135; Mentor, p. 166.

9 Everyman, p. 135; Mentor, p. 166.

10 *Meditation VI,* fifth paragraph (towards the end).

11 *Meditation VI*: Everyman, p. 134; Mentor, p. 166.

12 Stout, *op. cit.,* p. 196.

13 *Meditation VI,* tenth para.: Everyman, p. 134; Mentor, p. 165.

14 Stout, *loc. cit.*

15 Everyman, p. 134; Mentor, p. 166.

16 *Meditation. VI*: Everyman, p. 135; Mentor, p. 166.

17 See Everyman, pp. 135ff., Mentor, pp. 166ff., for the entire explanation that follows.

18 Cf. Stout, *op. cit.,* p. 198.

19 Everyman, p. 136; Mentor, p. 167.

[20] *Ibidem.*

[21] Stout, *op. cit.,* p. 198.

[22] *Ibidem.*

[23] *Meditation VI*: Everyman, p. 137; Mentor, p. 168.

[24] Cf. the fifteenth paragraph, bracketed explanation in Veitch's translation, *Meditation VI:* Everyman, p. 137.

Direct deceptions by nature occur when those special teachings of nature which have a purely biological purpose prove misleading practically. Stout, *op. cit.,* p. 198.

[25] Everyman, p. 140; Mentor, p. 170.

[26] For comments on the expression 'as if' here, see Margaret Dauler Wilson, *Descartes,* London, 1978, p. 208.

[27] *Meditation VI:* Everyman, p. 140.

[28] Everyman, p. 141; Mentor, p. 171.

[29] Mentor, pp. 171 - 172; Everyman, pp. 141 - 142.

[30] Everyman, p. 142; Mentor, p. 172.

[31] *Ibidem.* See also Wilson, *op. cit.,* pp. 28ff.

[32] All citations in the present work from Etienne Gilson's work - *Etudes ser le rõle de la pensée médiévale dans la formation du systéme Cartésiene,* J. Vrin, Paris, 1951 - are made on the basis of the translation provided by A. K. Stout in his own citations therefrom in his 'Descartes' Proof of the Existence of Matter', *Philosophy,* vol 1; 1961. As to the present citation: Gilson's work, p. 300; Stout's article, p. 201.

[33] Gilson's work, p. 204 note I; Stout's article, p. 202.

[34] *Ibidem.*

[35] *Ibidem.*

[36] *Ibidem.*

[37] Gilson's work, last paragraph but one on p. 303; Stout, *op. cit.,* p. 204 and also note 2 on the page.

[38] P. 205 of Stout's article.

39 As per Adam and Tannery's edition of the works of Descartes. As for Stout, his reference to Descartes' writings are mostly based on this edition. *Meditation VI* (latin version) is contained in vol. *VII* of this edition.

40 *Reply to Objection II, volume VII,* Adam and Tannery's edition, p. 135. Stout, *op. cit.*, p. 203 n.3.

41 In Chapter One.

42 See note 37 above (of the present chapter).

43 Cf. Stout, *op. cit.,* p. 203.

44 Cf. Note VII under Notes to the Everyman edition of Descartes' *A Discourse on Method, Etc.*, translated and edited by John Veitch, Dent, London, 1949, p. 252. The words to be considered are: 'The contrast indicated by these terms ["formally" and "eminently"] in this relation is in regard to the manner in which a cause is said to contain its effect. A cause, as the sum of perfection or reality of its effect, may contain this reality in either of two ways, and must in one of them'. The words 'in either of two ways, and must in one of them' show clearly that there is *no conceivable third way* in which the cause may contain the reality of the effect.

45 Stout, *op. cit.*, p. 20I n. 2.

46 Gilson's first account, p. 242; Stout, *op. cit.*, p. 203.

47 *Ibidem.*

48 As Stout puts it: 'the teaching of nature (that is, ultimately, of God, the cause of our natures) . . . .' *Ibid.,* p. 204.

49 The original expression: '*raisonnement spontané et naturel*' (Gilson's work, p. 304) See Stout, *op. cit.*, p. 201.

50 As Stout says: 'In fact, he [Gilson] does not seem clearly to distinguish the teaching of nature from that of the natural light (i.e., as involved in a rational argument). . . .'.
Ibid., p. 205.

51 Jonathan Bennett, *Learning from Six Philosophers: Descartes, Spinoza, Leibniz, Locke, Berkeley, Hume,* Volume 2, Clarendon, Oxford, first published 2001, in paperback 2003, sect. 186, p. 72.

[52] J. Cottingham, R. Stoothoff, and D. Murdoch, eds., *The Philosophical Writings of Descartes,* Cambridge University Press, 1984 - 5, 2; 89, 101.

[53] *Vide ibid.,* 2; 136.

[54] Bennett, *loc. cit.*

[55] *Meditation IV,* second paragraph, Mentor, p. 147.

[56] Cf. Bennett, *op. cit.,* pp. 72f.

[57] As cited by Bennett: *Principles of Philosophy,* part I, section 29.

[58] As cited by Bennett: *Principles of Philosophy,* part II, section 1.

[59] *Meditation III,* last para, but one: Mentor, p. 146; Everyman, p. 110.

[60] Bennett, *op. cit.,* p. 73.

[61] *Ibidem.*

[62] *Ibidem.*

CHAPTER THREE

AN EXAMINATION OF DESCARTES' 'PROOF'

3.1 Foreword

As far as can be judged from Descartes' own claims and actual procedure, his proof of the external world rests on the principle of causality as followed by him and on his appeal to the veracity of God. Accordingly, in order to estimate his 'proof' critically, it is necessary to examine the principle of causality used by him and his appeal to the veracity of God.

In Descartes' treatment of the subject, in connection with the additional arguments intended to supplement his 'proof', two conflicting views have come to be presented about what he understands by the expression 'my nature' - that is, about the nature of man[1]. Some discussion on this point is required, and is to be made in the final section of this chapter.

3.2 Critique of the Principle of Causality Adopted by Descartes

The principle of causality made use of[2] by Descartes may well be called, after Cottingham, the Causal Adequacy Principle[3]. According to it, there must be at least as much reality in the cause as in the effect. The words 'at least'[4] allow that the cause may contain more reality than the effect, and only disallow that the cause may contain less reality than it. If something X has the property F, the cause of X must have at least as much F-ness as X itself has. Descartes writes: '. . . .whence can the effect draw its reality if not from its cause ? And how could the cause communicate to it this reality unless it possessed it in itself ?'[5] In his *Second Replies,* Descartes treats the causal adequacy principle as a version of the fundamental principle, *ex nihilo nihil fit,* and defends it as such by saying:

> For if we admit that there is something in the effect that was not previously in the cause, we shall also have to admit that this something was produced by nothing.[6]

Descartes regards the causal principle as 'manifest by the natural light'[7], that is, as self-evident. What has to be examined, then, is whether the principle is really self-evident.

The causal principle is applied by Descartes to physical items as well as to the realm of ideas. Although our present concern is with his proof of the external world, where he applies the principle to some ideas - namely, sensory ideas, - its application to physical items must also be taken into account in a *general* assessment of the principle. For if this principle, when applied to physical items, be flawed, its application to the realm of ideas cannot be held to be above suspicion. Indeed, a principle which is claimed to be 'manifest by the natural light' cannot properly be regarded as such if, in its application to *any* realm, it be found to be untenable. It must be pointed out further that in *Meditation III,* where he applies the causal adequacy principle to the idea of God in order to determine the cause of this idea, he first of all seeks to explain the principle itself, and that, as he does this, he illustrates it by taking the example of physical items, such as stones[8]. And it is in *Meditation III* itself that he makes the claim that the principle is manifest by the natural light. This serves to strengthen our contention that Descartes' causal principle must be assessed in its dual application to the realm of ideas and the realm of physical effects.

3.2.1 Gassendi's criticism

The causal adequacy principle is meant by Descartes to apply to 'efficient' causes. Thus he says in *Meditation III:* '. . . . it is manifest by the natural light that there must at least be as much reality in the *efficient .... cause* as in the effect'[9]. As is well known, an efficient cause is the productive power or agency which brings something into being. But Gassendi has objected to Descartes' view on the ground that whatever plausibility the causal adequacy principle has belongs to it in so far as it is based on a consideration, not of efficient causes, but of 'material' causes, that is, ingredients[10]. To consider, for example, a bridge, which is very strong. It is, indeed, plausible to argue that the strength of the bridge is derived from the strength of its material ingredients, namely, girders, rivets, etc.

But though the case of material causation seems to be the favourable case for the causal adequacy principle, it is open to criticism, even in this case, as will be clear soon.

3.2.2 The difficulties of the causal adequacy principle as applied to material causes

As applied to material causes, the causal principle in question is open to some counter-examples. Thus, helium, which is formed by fusion from hydrogen, has properties which are not contained in the hydrogen.

Perhaps a commoner example is necessary, because an example taken from modern science may seem unfair to Descartes. Thus, a sponge cake may be considered[11]: it has a peculiar characteristic, *sponginess,* which did not belong to any of its material ingredients, namely, flour, butter, eggs, etc. It is a new or emergent property accruing to it from the chemical changes generated by the processes of mixing and baking. It would not do to say that the peculiar property of sponginess of the sponge cake was somehow *potentially* contained in its material ingredients on the ground that otherwise the cake would have got it simply out of nothing, which is absurd. To say this would not be in keeping with Descartes' own procedure. According to him, the perfections contained in the effect must be contained in the cause, not merely *potentially,* but *actually* (even though the perfections of the effect may, in some cases, be contained in the cause more eminently). Thus in his causal argument for the existence of God, he has argued in clear terms that the perfections representatively contained in the idea of God as found in the mind must be present in its cause, not just potentially but *actually*[12].

3.2.3 Difficulties of the causal adequacy principle as applied to efficient causes

To come now to 'efficient' causation: In this case the problem of the emergence of new properties is more acute than in that of material causation. Mersenne in this connection has cited the example of the emergence of life, taking the action of the sun and rain on the earth to be the efficient cause or productive force of the generation of life. He has argued that, if animal life can be produced by non-living forces, then 'it does happen that an effect may derive from its cause some reality, which is nevertheless not present in the cause'[13].

In his reply Descartes has made two separate points at the same time[14]:

First, animals which he regards *as only complex machines* have no properties which are not also present in inanimate bodies.

Secondly, since the causal principle under consideration is explicitly concerned with 'the efficient *and total* cause' of an effect, it is clear that if animals have properties which are not also present in the sun, rain, etc., then these things do not constitute the *total* efficient cause of animal life.[15]

With reference to the second reply, Cottingham observes: 'The trouble with this manoeuvre is that Descartes seems to be making his position immune from criticism by baldly denying the possibility of genuine emergent properties.'[16] The implication of this criticism is that Descartes is here making a controversial point. In his view, the evolutionary biologists must be wrong in admitting the possibility that consciousness may emerge from non-conscious forces. Whether or not they were right was a matter for debate in Descartes' time, and even long before. He was already quite familiar with the Greek atomists who had argued for such emergence, as his comments on Democritus in the *Principles of Philosophy* (Pt. IV, 202) go to suggest. The fact that Descartes in his reply to Mersenne has made only a controversial point appears to be sufficient to undermine his claim that the truth of his causal principle is 'manifest by the natural light'.

The point is that the causal principle in question is not *self-evidently* true.

3.2.4 On the application of the causal adequacy principle to the realm of ideas

Something must now be said on Descartes' application of his causal adequacy principle to the sphere of ideas. Among his contemporaries, there were some who needlessly objected to this sort of application. According to an objection in the First Set of Objections, an idea being only a subjective aspect of thought, and not an actual object needing a cause, it is preposterous to look for a cause for it: 'Why should I look for a cause of something which is not actual, and which is simply an empty label, a non-entity ?'[17] To this objection, Descartes' reply is indeed sound. He argues that, although an idea has no existence outside the intellect, a causal explanation of its having a certain representative content is very well needful.

But although the objection to Descartes' application of the causal adequacy principle to the realm of ideas is not sound, it does not follow that the principle itself is self-evident. That it is not so has already been seen. If the principle were to be manifest by the natural light, counter-examples to it in any of its realms of application could not be found. It is not that the principle was supposed to apply only to the realm of ideas. As seen before, he has sought to illustrate this principle by applying it to *physical entities* like 'stones' even in the context where he proceeds to extend its application to the realm of ideas. The conclusion to be drawn is that his treatment of the principle is far from satisfactory[18].

It emerges that in so far as his proof of the external world hinges on his causal adequacy principle, it rests on a weak foundation.

3.3 Critique of Descartes' Appeal to God in His Proof of the Existence of Material Things

To pass on now to consider Descartes' appeal to the veracity of God in his proof of the existence of material things.

3.3.1 A brief comparison of Descartes' view with that of Berkeley

Some critics have deemed it fit to make a slight comparison in this connection between the views of Descartes and Berkeley.[19] As has been seen, Descartes holds that, in view of our strong inclination to believe that our sensory ideas are caused by material things, the divine veracity would be impugned if it were supposed that those ideas were caused, not by material things, but by God acting by Himself or through an agent or agents, superior in rank to material things. As is well known, Berkeley, on the contrary, thinks that it is God who produces sensations or ideas in our minds, without there being material things, even though, in Berkeley's view, this does not make God a deceiver. To him the notion of our perceptual experiences being caused by material things is unintelligible.

By making a comparison of this sort, the critics of Descartes do not want to suggest that Berkeley's view is better than that of Descartes. They only want to stress that there is no sufficient reason behind the Cartesian fear that God will have to be represented as a deceiver if the causal source of our sensations be not located in one way rather than in another. This is to say that Descartes' argument for the existence of material things by his special manner of appealing to the veracity of God is not compelling.

3.3.2 A reasoned account of Descartes' appeal to God

There remains another point to make in reference to Descartes' appeal to God's veracity. Behind his belief in the divine veracity, there is the conviction that God exists. The latter conviction comes to him from his proof - that is, from what he regards as his proof - of the existence of God. In the *Replies to the Second Set of Objections* Descartes contends that an atheist 'cannot be certain that he is not being deceived on matters which seem to him very evident'[20], and maintains that the atheist 'will never be free of this doubt until he acknowledges that God exists'. Clearly, then, according to Descartes, the certainty that one is not being deceived is dependent on the recognition that God is not a deceiver, and this recognition in its turn is available only to those who acknowledge the existence of God. For - as Robert Stoothoff asks us to note here - it is only after proving the existence of God (in *Meditation III*) that Descartes presents the fact that God is not a deceiver,

> citing this fact as something recognized through 'contemplation of the true God' .... - such contemplation presumably being possible only for someone who knows that God exists, or who possesses the [adequate] idea of God which (so Descartes thinks) leads to the recognition of God's existence.[21]

One can easily appreciate here that the entire burden of Descartes' view to the effect that God is not a deceiver - that is, of his appeal to the veracity of God, and consequently of his other views which hinge, at crucial steps, on his appeal to the divine veracity - comes to fall ultimately on his claim or acknowledgement that God exists. This claim, in so far as it is made in *Meditation III,* derives its strength from the causal proof of the existence of God given there, and, in so far as it is repeated in *Meditation IV,* is further fortified (so at least he thinks) by another proof of God's existence, which later on, since Kant's time, has come to be known as the ontological proof. Ultimately, therefore, the entire burden of some of his important views is borne - so at least he thinks - by his proofs of the existence of God. This being so, it seems to be quite clear that, if reasons be found to cast doubts on his proofs of the existence of God, the cogency of his appeal to the veracity of God will be lost, and, accordingly, his proof of the existence of external, material things will come to be seen as being of dubious value.

In the same vein, S. V. Keeling in his book, *Descartes,* has been critical of Descartes. He writes :

> If we were prepared to grant .... [certain] things, namely: Descartes' causal principle, ... and the existence of a veracious God who is responsible for our native propensities, then his proof of the existence of a material world would seem to be cogent. But we have .... reasons to doubt at least the last of these propositions, so his demonstration that matter exists .... fails.[22]

3.3.2.1 Descartes' proofs of the existence of God examined briefly

As for Descartes' proofs of the existence of God, it may be observed that his causal proof in the *Third Meditation* is founded on his causal principle, as is well known[23]. His causal principle has already been brushed aside before in 3.2; so his causal proof of the divine existence can be discarded without more ado.

In his ontological proof offered in the *Fifth Meditation* Descartes has first distinguished between essence and existence, and then argued that in the case of God existence is inseparable from essence[24]. This means - if it is put in modern terminology - that existence is already built-in to the concept of an all-perfect being. But this way of arguing will hardly do. As Kant in one of his criticisms of the ontological argument observes: 'Whatever, . . . and however much, our concept of an object may contain, we must go outside it, if we are to ascribe existence to the object'[25]. In the case of an empirical object, we can go outside its concept through its connection with some one of our perceptions, in accordance with empirical laws. But in dealing with an object of pure thought, any supposed existence outside the realm of thought as ascribbd to the object thought through its concept is - in the absence of some extra-conceptual backing - 'of the nature of an assumption which we can never be in a position to justify'[26].

As the arguments lying behind Descartes' appeal to the veracity of God are found to be extremely weak, this appeal cannot be relied upon as a provider of philosophical warrant to any serious claim.

Accordingly, what Descartes has called his proof of the existence of material things cannot, in so far as it depends on his appeal to God, be regarded as a satisfactory proof.

Before bringing this chapter to a close, some critical observations need to be made on Descartes' conflicting views about the nature of man.

Although the conflict concerns only his views as to the nature of man, consideration of it cannot be out of place here, because the whole difficulty arises in connection with his arguments for the existence of an external world, as will be clear by and by.

3.4 On Descartes' Conflicting Views about What Is Meant by 'My Nature'

As to his nature - termed by him 'my nature', meaning man's nature - Descartes' central view is expressed in the *Meditations* in such a sentence as 'I am merely a thinking thing'[27]. In the eighth paragraph *of Meditation VI* he says: 'my essence consists only in my being a thinking thing'[28]. The word 'only' here is significant: it indicates that my body is not essential to me. In his *Discourse on Method* (1637) the point was put more clearly in this way :

> I concluded thence that I was a substance whose whole essence or nature consists only in thinking, and which, that it may exist, has need of no place, nor is dependent on any material thing; so that 'I' that is to say, the mind by which I am what I am, is wholly distinct from the body, and . . . . is such that, although the latter were not, it would still continue to be all that it is.[29]

The abovementioned view as to his (i.e. man's) nature is obtained by Descartes as he depends on the 'natural light' - that is, rational argument. But as he comes to listen to what he calls the 'dictates of nature', his view becomes noticeably different. Thus - as we may recall - he says in the twelfth paragraph of *Meditation VI*:

> Nature . . . . teaches me by these sensations of pain, hunger, thirst, etc., that I am not only lodged in my body as a pilot in a vessel, but that I am besides so intimately conjoined, and as it were intermixed with it, that my mind and body compose a certain unity.
>
> [Also cited before in Chapter Two]

It appears, then, that there is a contradiction in the Cartesian account between what the light of reason reveals to me about what I am, and what my sensory experience tells me about the same. It seems that, for Descartes, I am two incompatible things:

in the first place, I am purely incorporeal, only a thinking mind, as reason tells me; in the second place, I am *also* corporeal, partly corporeal, i.e. a compound of mind and body, as experience tells me.[30]

The contradiction was pointed out to Descartes in 1648 by Frans Burman. He quoted the passage, which we have last cited above, from the twelfth paragraph of *Meditation VI* and asked Descartes :

> how can this be, when [in your view] their natures [the nature of the mind and that of the body] are so completely different ?[31]

To this question raised by Burman, while interviewing Descartes, the latter replied as follows :

> This is very difficult to explain; but here our experience is sufficient, since it is so clear on this point that it just cannot be gainsaid.[32]

On Descartes' reply, Cottingham comments by saying that it is a lame reply, and explains why it is lame in the following words :

> The reply is lame because although the evidence of my inner sensory experience may, as Descartes says, be undeniable, the result it seems to lead us to (that I am an embodied creature) is incompatible with Descartes' central claim that I am essentially incorporeal.[33]

Whether the charge of self-conflict against Descartes' account of the nature of man could be obviated is a question which it is not easy to answer. In his eagerness to do justice to the claims of both rational argument and sensory experience, Descartes has not perhaps allowed himself to be fully consistent in his account of the nature of man. He is - we see - too big a philosopher for mere consistency. For our part, we have just noted the incompatibility pointed out by Burman between his (Descartes') two views concerning the nature of man, and are led to conclude that his account is not after all quite satisfactory.

To sum up: Descartes' proof of the external world has failed, because its twofold basis - the causal principle, and the force of the appeal to the veracity of God - has been undermined. His additional arguments, intended to supplement his 'proof', are indeed an excellent source of information for us on many points, but have, by bringing in a view as to the nature of man, come into conflict with his central view regarding that. So the conclusion becomes unavoidable that his proof under examination has not been successful.

As per the plan of this work, it is time to proceed next to study Kant's proof or proofs of the external world, as given in the *Critique of Pure Reason.*

NOTES

1 As Descartes writes in the first person, he is obliged to use an expression like 'my nature', although he means *human* nature. The title, e.g., *of Meditation II* – 'Of the Nature of the Human Mind; . . . .' - is noteworthy, as showing that he is concerned with *what is human,* and not with what is true of an individual personally and exclusively. The clarificatory addition of the phrase 'of man' to the title of *Meditation VI* in the subsequent French version of 1647 - 'the Existence of Material Things, and the Real Distinction between the Mind and Body of Man' - may here be referred to as confirming further that the expression 'my nature' in the Cartesian usage has the ultimate significance of *man's nature.*

2 The principle of causality under reference is not propounded for the first time by Descartes; it is only used by him after borrowing it essentially from the schoolmen.

3 John Cottingham, *Descartes,* Basil Blackwell, Oxford, 1986, p. 49.

4 *Meditation III,* eleventh para; Mentor, p. 138.

5 *Ibidem.*

6 *The Philosophical Writings of Descartes,* trans. J. Cottingham, R. Stoothoff, and D. Murdoch, Cambridge University Press, 1985, vol. 2, p. 97. See also Cottingham, *Descartes,* p. 49.

7 *Meditation III:* Mentor, 138; Everyman, 100.

8 *Meditation III:* Mentor, 138; Everyman, 100-101.

9 Italics added. Mentor, 138; Everyman, 100.

10 *Philosophical Writings,* vol. 2, p. 201. Cf. also Cottingham, *op. cit.,* (1986) p. 51.

11 *Ibidem.*

12 In *Meditation III* (see Everyman, p. 106; Mentor, pp. 142f), Descartes says: 'But I conceived God as actually infinite, ... And . . . . I readily perceive that the objective being of an idea cannot be produced by a being that is merely potentially existent, which, properly speaking, is nothing, but only by a being existing . . . . actually'. It is noteworthy that, for him, what is 'merely potentially existent' is as good as 'nothing'. He seems to be thinking along the following line :

If a cause were to contain a reality or perfection merely potentially, it would require something *additional* for the actualization of what is so contained in it. But then a second cause would be necessary. And thus complications would arise.

In other words: if a cause were to contain potentially a reality which is actually found in the effect, then the cause would contain less than the effect, and this is absurd.

13 *Philosophical Writings,* vol. *2,* p. 88. Also Cottingham, *loc. cit.*

14 *Ibidem.*

15 *Ibid.,* p. 52. [As for Descartes' phrase 'the efficient and total cause', See also *Meditation III:* Mentor, 138.]

16 Cottingham, *loc. cit.*

17 *Philosophical Writings,* vol. 2, p. 67; cited by Cottingham, *Descartes,* p. 52.

18 The causal principle adopted by Descartes has been criticized very variously by critics. Sec for example:

A. Boyce Gibson, *The Philosophy of Descartes,* Methuen, London, 1932, pp. 110-124; B. Williams, *Descartes: The Project of Pure Enquiry,* Humanities Press, 1978, pp. 138-141, 142f.; Margaret Dauler Wilson, *Descartes,* Routledge & Kegan Paul, London, 1978, pp. 137f.

19 See, for example, Williams, *op. cit.,* ch. 8, p. 233 n. 12.

20 *Philosophical Writings,* vol. 2, p. 101.

21 Robert Stoothoff, 'Descartes Dilemma', in *The Philosophical Quarterly,* vol. 39, No. 156, July 1989, Basil Blackwell, p. 304 [of pp. 294-307].

22 S. V. Keeling, *Descartes,* 2nd edn, Oxford University Press, London, 1968, p. 278.

23 Descartes' causal proof for the existence of God involves indeed two arguments. The first argument is expressly dependent on the causal adequacy principle, and is accordingly liable to be rejected on the ground pointed out in the text. As for the second argument, it raises certain complications. There are some commentators who treat it as a distinct proof and judge it in that light; See, for example, E. M. Curley, *Descartes against the Sceptics,* Blackwell, Oxford, 1978, pp. 138ff. Descartes' own

view, with regard to the second argument as compared with the first, is, however, that it is not a distinct proof, but rather a further development of the line of reasoning presented in the first; thus in the First Set of Replies he says: "I went on to inquire [in the second argument] "whether I could exist if God did not exist". But my purpose here was not to produce a different proof from the preceding one, but rather to take the same proof and provide a more thorough explanation of it.' See *The Philosophical Writings of Descartes,* vol. 2, p. 31. As concerns us, the more important question is not whether the second argument is, or is not, a distinct proof, but is whether it, like the first, depends on the causal adequacy principle. To this question an affirmative reply must be given, as can be confirmed by a reference to *Meditation III* {*Philosophical Writings* vol. 2, p. 31, Mentor, p. 144, 2nd para.). This being so, the second argument is, like the first, equally liable to rejection on the ground pointed out in the text.

24 See the argument which starts in, and is carried forward from, the third paragraph of *Meditation V.*

25 *Critique of Pure Reason,* A601 = B629, on p. 506, 2nd para., in Kemp Smith's translation.

26 *Ibidem.*

27 *Meditation VI* : Mentor, p. 166; Everyman, p. 135. A sentence of the sort under reference occurs several times in the *Meditations* from *Meditation II* onwards.

28 Mentor, p. 164; Everyman, p. 132; *Philosophical Writings,* vol. 2, p. 54.

29 *Discourse,* Part IV: Everyman, p. 27; *Philosophical Writings,* vol. 1, p. 127.
We have written the short title of Descartes work under reference as 'Discourse on Method' by following the usual practice, even though we are aware of Cottingham's note in his *Descartes,* p. 2I n. 20: 'The correct short title in English is *Discourse on the Method;* the common rendering "Discourse on Method" is indefensible since it makes nonsense of the full title. The title of Descartes' most famous work has an unfortunate history of being misquoted: a French government commemorative stamp issued in 1950 to mark the tercentenary of Descartes' death depicted a book entitled "Discours *sur* la méthode".'

Be it noted here that in the Everyman's Library edition the short title is *A Discourse on Method.*

30 Cf. Cottingham, 'Descartes, *Sixth Meditation'*, in Vesey, ed., *Philosophers, Ancient and Modern,* p. 87.

31 Burman's question, and Descartes' reply, are from *Descartes' Conversation with Burman,* trans, and ed. J. Cottingham, Clarendon, 1976, p. 28.

32 See note 31 above.

33 See Cottingham's article in Vesey, *loc. cit.*

CHAPTER FOUR

KANT'S PROOF OF THE EXISTENCE OF EXTERNAL THINGS IN SPACE (AS GIVEN IN THE FIRST EDITION OF THE 'CRITIQUE OF PURE REASON')

4.1 Foreword

In the first as well as in the second edition of the *Critique of Pure Reason* Kant has given us a proof of the existence of empirically external things, because he thinks that Descartes' so-called proof of their existence is not satisfactory. His first-edition proof occurs in the course of his discussion of the fourth *Paralogism* (A 366 - 80), and his second-edition proof in the new section, *Refutation of Idealism,* at B 274-79. His proofs in question are sometimes referred to by commentators as his first-edition refutation, and as his second-edition refutation, of idealism[1]. 'Idealism' in this connection means the problematic idealism of Descartes, that is, the Cartesian scepticism[2]. Kant's proofs of the existence of external, material, things find articulations through his refutations of problematic or sceptical idealism. His intention behind his proofs under reference is throughout to defeat scepticism about the external, material, world. It is, therefore, all the same whether we refer to what he has done at the two places as his 'proofs' of the existence of external, material, things or as his 'refutations' of the Cartesian scepticism about the same.

In the present chapter, as is indicated in its subtitle, we are concerned with Kant's first-edition proof of the existence of empirically external things. We start with his direct criticism of the Cartesian causal inference which he comes to regard as a precarious inference, because, in his view, it tends to make the existence of empirically external things doubtful and thus fails to render it certain. We thence proceed, through clarifications of preliminaries, to his 'proof' and study it in detail with due attention to the interpretative issues involved in it.

4.2 Kant's Direct Criticism of Descartes' Causal Inference of the Existence of Empirically External Things

While studying Descartes, we have seen that, for him, the immediate contents of perception are some sensory ideas, while external, corporeal, objects are not immediately given as objects of perception[3]. So he seeks to prove their existence by *inferring* them as external causes of our sensory ideas.

Kant, towards the end of A367 of the *Critique of Pure Reason*, refers to Descartes by name, and proceeds, at the beginning of A368, to state his (i.e. Descartes') position in the following words :

> I am not . . . . in a position to *perceive* external things, but can only infer their existence from my inner perception, taking the inner perception as the effect of which something external is the proximate cause.[4]

After stating Descartes' position in the above way - and this way of stating the position is surely quite in keeping with Descartes' actual procedure, as should be amply clear from our previous exposition of his view - , Kant comes to hold that a causal inference of the Cartesian sort is *inconclusive*, as it has to be[5]. He says that 'the inference from a given effect to a determinate cause is always uncertain, since the effect may be due to more than one cause'[6]. Kant develops his criticism by way of arguing:

> Accordingly, as regards the relation of the perception to its cause, it always remains doubtful whether the cause be internal or external; whether, that is to say, all the so-called outer perceptions are not a mere play of our inner sense, or whether they stand in relation to actual external objects as their cause. At all events, the existence of the latter is only inferred[7], and is open to all the dangers of inference. . . . .[8]

The gist of the Kantian contention is that one can never be sure of having excluded all alternative causes before hitting upon the exact cause. Following Paton, we may try to explain this point by means of an example :

Descartes, while considering the question whether the cause of our sensory ideas is internal or not, has considered and rejected the possibility that we ourselves are *consciously* the cause of such ideas, but has not even thought of excluding the possibility that we ourselves are *unconsciously* their cause. As Paton puts the point :

> In this particular case it is possible that we are ourselves unconsciously the cause of our ideas, just as we are consciously the cause of our ideas when we indulge in arbitrary imagination.[9]

This example is given only in order to enforce the Kantian contention that the Cartesian causal inference remains inconclusive and doubtful. Indeed, one can never be sure, in such an approach, that all alternative explanations have been considered and excluded.[10]

The question arises: How does Kant for himself avoid the problem of inconclusive inference ? How, in other words, does he himself seek to prove, in the first edition of the *Critique*, the existence of external things in space ?

4.3 Preparing to Approach Kant's First-Edition Proof of the Existence of External Things in Space

Kant for himself avoids the problem of inconclusive inference by arguing that, in so far as we claim to know that there are external objects, we claim to know that there are *spatial objects*, and that we know of spatial objects primarily in virtue of an immediate representation, that is, intuition.[11]

Space, according to Kant, is a form of outer (that is, external) intuition[12], in the sense that what is intuited in this form is intuited *outwardly* - not inwardly. An external object, as an object outside us, is, then, an object *in space*. In this usage, externality is understood by Kant in terms of spatiality.[13]

There is, however, another usage in which the expression 'outside us' has also a sense, for Kant. In this sense, the term is applicable to things in themselves in his philosophy. Things in themselves are, for him, outside us, not in the sense of spatial objects (like chairs, tables, mountains, etc.), but in the sense of things lying apart from us[14], quite independently of our conditions of knowledge. As lying quite independently of our conditions of knowledge, they are, for Kant, unknown and unknowable, even though not inconceivable or unthinkable by us.

In so far as the phrase 'outside us', or 'external to us', is applicable to things in themselves, Kant chooses to mark this sense of externality by calling it *externality in the transcendental sense*, whereas externality in the sense of spatiality is called by him *externality in the empirical sense*[15].

We have to quote now a passage, where Kant has pointed out the ambiguity of 'outside us', and given us an implicit instruction as to how the nature of the problem before us is to be defined. For it will then be easier for us to appreciate properly the line taken by him to solve the problem.

The passage under reference is this :

> The expression *'outside us'* is thus unavoidably ambiguous in meaning, sometimes signifying what *as thing in itself* exists apart from us, and sometimes what belongs solely to outer *appearance.* In order, therefore, to make this concept, in the latter sense - the sense in which the psychological question as to the reality of our outer intuition has to be understood - quite unambiguous, we shall distinguish *empirically external* objects from those which may be said to be external in the transcendental sense, by explicitly entitling the former *'things which are to be found in space'.* [A 373]

a. Defining the nature of the problem at hand

Our present concern is with Kant's proof of the existence of external things (as given in the first edition of the *Critique).* Clearly, in this context, external things are, for Kant, external in the sense of empirically external things, such as chairs, tables, mountains, and other corporeal things. Empirically external things are by him understood - as has already been pointed out - in the sense of *spatial objects.* Thus, the problem of proving the existence of external things is understood by him as the problem of proving the existence of spatial objects.

b. How Kant addresses himself to the problem

As for spatial objects, these are, in Kant's view, objects which are given, or capable of being given, in space. Since 'given' means *intuited*[16], it is clear that spatial objects are, or can be, *intuited in space.* They are intuited in space empirically, even though space itself is, for him, intuited *a priori*[17]. Kant explains this by saying that the *a priori* intuition of space is possible (that is, intelligible)[18] in so far as space is a form - that is, a condition[19] - of empirical intuition. Objects which are intuited empirically come to be intuited spatially, because space is a form or condition, or a way, of empirical intuition.(We are here ignoring time for the present purpose).[20] In the total intuitional situation, there is a spatial element[21], and there are non-spatial elements. The spatial element has been intuited *a priori,* and the non-spatial elements (except the temporal element ignored here for the sake of convenience) have been intuited empirically. This is the Kantian analysis of the intuitional situation, and the analysis has been presented here in an incomplete way, because further details about it do not concern us for our present purposes.

To come to the point. The point is that external objects, in the sense of spatial objects, are, for Kant, such that they are initially *given,* that is, immediately apprehended. The word 'initially'[22] is here added, because there is also the role of conceptualization in the knowledge of spatial objects. As given or immediately represented initially, however, they resist any Cartesian sort of wonder whether they exist. On the immediate evidence of intuition, their existence is sufficiently proved, according to Kant.[23]

In support of the above, some textual evidence is perhaps required.

Textual Evidence

It will do to cite only the following passages :

> [i] Space and time are indeed *a priori* representations, which dwell in us as forms of sensible intuition, ... But the material [i.e. the non-formal] or real element, the something which is to be intuited in space, necessarily presupposes perception. [A 373]
>
> [ii] This perception, ... (to consider, for the moment, only outer intuitions), represents something real in space.

> For .... while space is the representation of a mere possibility of co-existence, perception is the representation of a reality....
> [If the presentatum in space] were not real, that is, immediately given through empirical intuition, it could not be pictured in imagination, since what is real in intuitions cannot be invented *a priori*. [A 374 - 75]
>
> [iii] All outer perception, therefore, yields immediate proof of something real in space, ... [A 375]

Kant on deceptive illusions

Kant is aware that for his view there are difficulties arising from the fact of illusions, delusions, dreams, etc. He has observed, however, that such deceptive representations can always be dealt with in terms of empirical criteria. He admits[24] that from perceptions there may arise no doubt deceptive representations to which no actual objects correspond, but explains them as being due to either errors of judgment (in the so-called deceptions of the senses), or to delusions of imagination (in dreams). He holds that these can be corrected, or detected, by following the rule: 'Whatever is connected with a given perception in accordance with empirical laws, is actual.'[25]

Before proceeding further, we may compare Kant's view with that of Descartes to see how the Kantian proof of the existence of external things, as expounded so far, stands in relation to the Cartesian proof.

As may be recalled, Descartes has denied that external, spatial, objects are immediately given in perception. That is why, he had to resort to an inference, from some given ideas to them as causes, in his attempt to prove their existence. Kant, in his turn, however, has made this inference quite unnecessary, by presenting a unique theory of intuition, and by restoring, on the basis of this theory, the *immediacy* which was denied by Descartes to the original representation of spatial objects. As Kant's proof is a proof in terms of immediacy, he called it an *immediate proof*[26], while Descartes' proof was an inferential proof.

So far Kant's proof in the first edition has been considered without any *explicit* mention of the standpoint of transcendental idealism-cum-empirical realism from which in fact he has presented it in his *'Critique of the Fourth Paralogism'.* It is time now to turn to that side of the proof.

4.4 Consideration of Kant's First-Edition 'Proof' from the Standpoint of His Transcendental Idealism-cum-Empirical Realism

It will be well to start, for this purpose, with A. C. Ewing's summary of what he calls 'the main argument of the first edition refutation'[27].

4.4.1 Kant's main argument (in Ewing's terms)

Ewing's statement of the Kantian argument follows :

First Edition (A 370-I). I am immediately aware of my representations.

> Physical objects are only a species *(Art)* of my representations.
>
> ∴ I am immediately aware of physical objects.
>
> ∴ Physical objects are known with certainty to exist.[28]

Ewing, however, has made no serious attempt to explain the above argument. Particularly the second sentence, saying that physical objects are only a species of representations, stands badly in need of a proper interpretation, if misunderstanding is to be avoided. What we propose to do is to consult Kant's own words, as translated by Kemp Smith, and to study them *in their context.*

For here the context is important. We may consider first Kant's own statement to the effect that material things are merely representations, and try to provide the required explanation in the light of the context.

4.4.2 On Kant's view that matter is only a species of representations

Kant says:

The transcendental idealist . . . . may be . . . . a *dualist*[29]; that is, he may admit the existence of matter without . . . . assuming anything more than the certainty of his representations . . . . For he considers this matter and even its inner possibility to be an appearance merely; and appearance, if separated from our sensibility, is nothing. Matter is with him, therefore, only a species of representations (intuition), which are called external, ... because they only relate perceptions to the space in which all things are external to one another, while yet the space itself is in us. [A 370]

The word 'representations', in the present context, means *ideas.* As is clear from the context, the Kantian view that material things are only a species of representations or ideas is to be taken, not in the ordinary sense of the term 'ideas', but in the transcendental-idealist sense of the term.

Transcendental idealism is a doctrine which regards all appearances, that is, objects of possible experience, including external physical objects, as 'representations only'. In the following passage Kant says this clearly :

> . . . . By *transcendental idealism* I mean the doctrine that appearances are to be regarded as being, one and all, representations, not things in themselves, and that time and space are therefore only sensible forms of our intuition, not determinations given as existing by

> themselves, nor conditions of objects viewed as things in themselves.[30]

But on what grounds does Kant regard *all* appearances - and so external objects in space - as *representations* only ?

> Something like an answer to this is obtainable in the following passage :
>
> We have sufficiently proved in the Transcendental Aesthetic that everything intuited in space or time, and therefore all objects of any experience possible to us, are nothing but appearances, that is, mere representations, which, in the manner in which they are represented, as extended beings, or as series of alterations, have no independent existence outside our thoughts. This doctrine I entitle *transcendental idealism.*
>
> [**An exegetical note** : here the clause 'have no independent existence outside our thoughts' should be reconstructed as 'have no independent existence outside our sensibility'. Mark Kant's reference to 'our sensibility' two sentences later on in the same passage.[31]]

Now in this latter passage Kant is saying that appearances can be regarded as mere representations in virtue of *the manner in which they are represented.* They are represented spatially and temporally, or, as in some cases, only temporally: (spatially and temporally, in the case of outer appearances, and only temporally, in the case of inner appearances). The spatial or temporal way of representing is only *our* (that is, 'human')[32] way of representing (or intuiting); and this is so, because Kant has shown in the Transcendental Aesthetic that space and time are only forms, i.e. ways, of our sensibility. As such, space and time, and with them, appearances[33]- even outer appearances - are, for him, 'mere representations'. He sometimes otherwise puts the point by saying that they are 'in us'[34]. They are said to be *in us* in order merely to emphasize their subject-dependence, to use this phrase of Sebastian Gardner's[35]. They are essentially subject-dependent, in so far as they are inseparably connected with our sensibility. As Kant says, as we have seen: 'appearance, if separated from our sensibility, is nothing'. What is meant is that if their relation to our sensibility is disregarded, they do not remain over as things in themselves, or as belonging to things in themselves.

As one can see now, the force of Kant's claim that space, time, and even outer appearances are mere representations or ideas lies ultimately in his insistence that these things are neither things in themselves nor any determinations of things in themselves. Now, as G. Bird observes, 'to rely on the distinction between things in themselves and things as appearances is to employ a transcendental, and not empirical, distinction'[36]. So it is clear that Kant's claim that these things are mere representations or ideas is only a transcendental claim, which cannot be understood except in terms of his transcendental idealism.

In terms of transcendental idealism, they are *ideas* in the sense of being transcendentally *ideal.* To claim that they are 'transcendentally ideal, or ideas in a transcendental sense' ;[37] is to claim that they exist, not quite independently of us, as a transcendental realist like Descartes supposes that they do, but as closely related to our sensibility. A natural objection to this interpretation is that although Kant talks of the transcendental ideality of space and time, he does not similarly talk in clear terms of the ideality of appearances. Bird answers this objection by conceding first that Kant talks of the ideality of space and time much more often than of the ideality of appearances, bur he (Bird) hastens to point out that it would be wrong to think that in the *Critique* there is no passage at all where Kant clearly talks of the ideality of appearances.[38] In the following passage cited by Bird from A 507 = B 535 Kant clearly refers to the transcendental ideality of appearances :

> .... From this it then follows that appearances in general are nothing outside our representations - which is what is meant by their transcendental ideality.

Some other passages in which Kant talks of the ideality of appearances can also be easily cited.[39] But it is not perhaps necessary to do that.

To revert now to external, material, objects, with which we are concerned. The apparent difficulty besetting the Kantian observation that matter is only a species of representations vanishes as soon as we give up here the ordinary meaning of 'representations' or 'ideas', and adopt, instead, the transcendental-idealistic meaning (as before explained). Material things are not ideas in the ordinary sense of mental states, because mental states are only intuited inwardly, and never outwardly, whereas material things, as spatial objects are only intuited outwardly. Kant, as an empirical dualist, adheres to the ordinary conviction which discriminates between the physical and the mental. This distinction coincides, for him, with the distinction between the outer and the inner. He maintains that what is outer is represented in space, and what is inner is represented only in time. As he puts it: '*external* .... if it is represented *in space ;* and *inner* .... if it is represented only *in its time-relations*'[40]. It is clear that the term 'representations' in the Kantian observation that material things, that is, spatial objects, are only a species of representations is not used in the ordinary sense of mental states. And it has been already made clear that the term is there used in the transcendental sense[41], which signifies that they are merely appearances, i.e. are not, or do not belong to, things in themselves quite independently of our sensibility.

Since we are concerned in this chapter with Kant's proof (in the first edition) of the existence of external, material, things, it is now time to pass on to it, and try to see what bearing his view that matter is 'only a species of representations (intuition)' has on the proof.

4.4.3 Explaining Kant's first-edition proof of the existence of physical objects, i.e. of material things

Kant, as a transcendental idealist *cum* empirical realist, is committed to proving not only 'the existence of matter', but also the existence of it 'without going outside his mere self-consciousness, or assuming anything more than the certainty of his representations'. [Cf. his opening sentence on page 370 at A of the *Critique*.] This is, obviously, a difficult task; and so we want to carry out our explanation of his 'proof' at two stages instead of trying to do so at only one stage.

4.4.3.1 Stage 1 : Explaining Kant's 'main argument' by resuming consideration of Ewing's statement of it

Kant's argument, which is called his 'main argument' in the first edition by Ewing, for the conclusion that physical objects, that is, material things, exist has already been presented by us before (at 4.4.2 above) in Ewing's terms. Reserving further comments on Ewing's version of the Kantian argument, we beg permission to quote it again for the sake of keeping it quite before our eyes to facilitate further discussion. The steps in the argument are now numbered by us for convenience of subsequent reference :

'[1] I am immediately aware of my representations.

[2] Physical objects are only a species of my representations.

[3] ∴ I am immediately aware of physical objects.

[4] ∴ Physical objects are known with certainty to exist.'

We presume that Ewing in the above sentences has sought to capture the spirit of the following sentences - also numbered by us - in Kant's own presentation of the argument concerned :

> '[i] I am conscious of my representations; these representations, and I myself, who have the representations, therefore exist.' [*Critique,* A 370]
>
> '[ii] External objects (bodies), however, are mere appearances, and are nothing but a species of my representations, ...' [*Ibidem*]
>
> '[iii] Thus external things exist as well as I myself, and both, indeed, upon the immediate witness of my self-consciousness.' [*Ibid.,* A 371]

The differences between the above two presentations - one in Ewing's terms and the other in Kant's own - of the Kantian argument for the existence of physical objects, or material things, on the immediate evidence of our consciousness, that is, by an appeal to immediate apprehension, does not here matter much. Hence Ewing's presentation of the Kantian argument concerned for the existence of matter on the evidence of intuition (i.e. immediate awareness) is, as a *statement* of the argument, fairly dependable. Indeed, he has done us a great service by briefly and neatly and fairly correctly stating Kant's main argument for the existence of matter - an argument which would otherwise have escaped our notice. But he (Ewing) has done nothing to *explain* Kant's argument itself - particularly the crucial steps involved in it, taking them one after another. So trouble is waiting for us, again.

Step (2) in Ewing's presentation, which corresponds to step (ii) in Kant's own presentation, of the argument under study appeared at first to be quite puzzling. There can be no denying that the Kantian statement of the sort, 'Physical objects are only a species of my representations', is extremely puzzling if the word 'representations' in it is taken, as it is only too natural to take it, in the ordinary sense of *mental states.* By a close study of the text and of the context, however, we have come to see that the word in question in 'Material things - physical objects - are only a species of my representations' is intended by Kant to be taken, not in the sense of *mental states,* but in the transcendental sense of *appearances,* signifying that these things or objects are not, and do not belong to, things in themselves quite independently of our sensibility. But now a fresh difficulty arises, as we turn our attention to step (1.) in Ewing's statement, which corresponds to step (i) in Kant's own statement, of the argument before us. This fresh difficulty may be spelled out as follows :

In the first step of the argument Kant's statement, 'I am conscious of my representations', is paraphrased by Ewing as 'I am immediately aware of my representations'. This is a correct paraphrase, indeed. For the context of the Kantian argument before us happens to be one in which Kant is talking in terms of *immediate* consciousness. The words 'upon the immediate witness of my self-consciousness', which occur in the last clause of the last-quoted passage from the *Critique,* and which in the context mean the same as 'on the immediate evidence of my self-consciousness', are noteworthy. What is more, the paragraph (not fully quoted above by us) in which Kant's argument under consideration occurs has at the end of it the words: 'the immediate perception (consciousness) of which is at the same time a sufficient proof of their reality'[42]. There can be no question therefore that Kant's argument in proof of the existence of external things (bodies) rests on an appeal to the evidence of immediate perception (consciousness). The rationale of such an appeal will be clear, as we proceed. We must hasten to come back to the point: In the first step of his argument before us, we have seen that Kant says, 'I am conscious of my representations', which allows, in virtue of the context, of being taken, in Ewing's way, as 'I am immediately conscious of my representations'. The question arises as to the sense in which the expression 'my representations' used in it is to be taken. Obviously, the expression here has a natural claim to be taken in the sense of *my mental states.* It is, indeed, very natural to say, as many say, that I am immediately conscious of my mental states. But, then, a serious difficulty arises, if not for Kant's statement itself in the first step, at least in respect of the validity of his argument before us. It has already been seen that the self-same expression 'my representations' used in the second step of the argument is to be taken - or rather, demands to be taken - not, in the ordinary empirical sense of *my mental states,* but in a different sense (in the transcendental sense of *appearances).* This being so, it strongly seems to be the case that in his argument the conclusion is arrived at fallaciously, *per sophisma figurae dictions* - that is, through an ambiguous employment of the key-expression 'representations' in the premises.

The abovementioned difficulty can be resolved along the Kantian line in the following way. [We must give here, *in advance,* a brief idea of what we are going to make out: Even if the term 'representations' in the first premise of the Kantian argument for the existence of matter is taken in the ordinary sense of mental states, it has still a transcendental-idealist signification in the final analysis.] To proceed step by step along the Kantian line, starting with the mental states :

(a) My mental states, for Kant, are only inner states. Inner states, such as sensory states (e.g. the sensory ideas talked of by Descartes), are, in Kant's view, temporal occurrents, and are, precisely for this reason, called inner. Such states are represented - intuited - in time, only in time, not also in space. As Kant puts it: 'an inner state stands under the formal condition of inner intuition, and so belongs to time'[43]. This is to say that inner sensory states are necessarily subject to time which is the form of inner sense. He has not simply assumed, but rather established on the basis of arguments in the Transcendental Aesthetic, that time 'is nothing but the form of inner sense, that is, of the intuition of ourselves and of our inner state'[44]. The result achieved so far is only that inner sensory states are necessarily involved in time. (b) Now, with regard to time the view finally reached by Kant in the Transcendental Aesthetic is: 'Time is .... a purely subjective condition of our (human) intuition. . . , and in itself, apart from the subject, is nothing'[45]. This being so, our inner sensory states, which are necessarily involved in time, are purely subjective, not merely in the ordinary empirical sense, but, more importantly, in the transcendental sense of being essentially subject-dependent. (c) As being thus essentially subject-dependent, inner states are called by Kant *appearances* (in his technical sense), and specifically characterized by him as 'inner appearances'.[46] (d) Now, *all* appearances - both outer and inner appearances - are, for Kant, mere representations; thus, he says at A 379 : '. . . . we take inner and outer appearances together as mere representations . . . .' Obviously, the term 'representations' here is to be taken in the transcendental-idealist sense of being *in us,* that is, in the sense of being *necessarily dependent on our sensibility*[47]. We here arrive at the result we wanted to come by. There remains the task of making clear to ourselves what our net achievement has been, so far as our main objective behind mentioning the above points is concerned.

Kant has shown by a step-by-step analysis of the very notion of mental states that they are ultimately only appearances of a kind, and, as such, mere representations in the transcendental-idealist sense that they are necessarily dependent on our sensibility. This is how his analysis has proceeded: mental states are only inner states occurring in time, and, as time is an appearance, inner states are also appearances of a kind, and appearances of any kind, being not things in themselves, are *mere representations* in the transcendental-idealist sense, signifying their essential subject-dependence. Thus the transcendental-idealist sense of 'representations' becomes in the end inescapable.

Reverting to the term 'representations' in Kant's first premise in his argument for the existence of matter, namely, 'I am [immediately] conscious of my representations', we can now straightway put on that term a transcendental-idealist construction, upon which it only stands for essentially subject-dependent items or objects. What Kant calls 'objects of the senses' - objects of inner sense only, and objects of outer sense also - are items or objects of this sort. It is only if objects are essentially subject-dependent (more precisely: formally dependent on our sensibility) that the subject can be *immediately* conscious of them - i.e. can have an immediate cognitive access to them. This immediate cognitive access to objects is called in the Transcendental Aesthetic 'intuition': 'In whatever manner and by whatever means a mode of knowledge may relate to objects, *intuition* is that through which it is in immediate relation to them, and to which all thought as a means is directed'. (A 19) At 371 he calls it 'immediate perception' (consciousness): 'Perception here signifies 'empirical intuition'; cf. A 375.

Adoption of the transcendental-idealist interpretation of the term 'representation' used in the first premise of Kant's argument for the existence of matter has two notable advantages :

First, it brings the interpretation of the term 'representation' in Kant's first premise into line with that which has already been put before on the self-same term occurring in the second premise.

Secondly, - and consequently - it can now be said that Kant's argument in question does not depend upon an ambiguous employment of the key-term in his expression 'my representation' in his two premises - whether we take his own, or Ewing's, version of it. At first it no doubt seems that the argument depends upon a sort of equivocation on the term 'representations'. But the above discussion has shown that the argument does not really involve the *fallacy of equivocation.*

The first and second steps in Kant's argument for the existence of matter (physical or material things) have been explained so far. From these two steps, the third step (which is Kant's first conclusion, according to Ewing) follows logically. But the transition from the third step in the argument to the fourth step (yielding us ultimately Kant's main conclusion) requires some explanation. On this point at least Ewing has been for us helpful. The explanation given by him is as follows :

> We have, however, hardly mentioned [or rather, not properly explained] a point on which Kant laid great stress. He wished not only to justify the belief in physical objects but to do so in a way which would finally get rid of the representative theory of perception. In the first edition refutation he argues that, since physical objects are only my representations, I must perceive them immediately; .... Kant thought this an important contribution chiefly because it removed any possible theoretical doubt about the existence of physical objects, whereas the doubt might always recur if it were admitted that we did not perceive them immediately. Kant assumes that if they are perceived immediately they are known immediately, and that conversely we cannot know them immediately unless we perceive them immediately.[48]

This explanation would be accepted as quite satisfactory if we were allowed to modify certain sentences in it. Thus, in the light of what we have said before, we should like to modify Ewing's third sentence ('In the first edition refutation .... them immediately') as follows :

> In the first edition refutation he [Kant] argues that, since physical objects, as appearances, are only representations [in the transcendental-idealist sense of being necessarily

> - formally - dependent on our sensibility], we can well [our sensibility can well] perceive them immediately.

And Ewing's last sentence ('Kant assumes . . . perceive them immediately') requires, in the light of Kant's actual position in the *Critique*, to be modified as follows:

> Kant holds that if they are perceived immediately we can be certain that they exist, and that we cannot be certain that they exist unless we either perceive them immediately or (in, e.g., the cases in which they are not immediately perceived) have grounds to think that they are connected with some given perceptions according to empirical laws, our rule being [cf. A 376]: *'Whatever is connected with a perception according to empirical laws, is actual.'*

4.4.3.2 Stage 2: explaining the Kantian defence of the view that material things can be immediately perceived

Kant says :

> The transcendental idealist is, therefore, an empirical realist, and allows to matter, as appearance, a reality which does not permit of being inferred, but is immediately perceived.[49]

In this passage Kant suggests that only a transcendental idealist is able to advocate empirical realism according to which material things can be *immediately perceived,* and so need not be left at the mercy of any inconclusive causal inference from our sensory ideas. To appreciate this view clearly, it is necessary to consider Descartes' view once more.

Descartes treats of material things - or, as he calls them, corporeal things - as things existing quite independently of us. As existing quite independently of us, they exist quite independently of our senses. They are not, therefore, objects of the senses, in his view. So we are not surprised to see that he does not regard material things as available to us in immediate perception. He does not regard them as proper objects of immediate perception. The only immediate objects of perception he has been able to recognize are certain sensory contents. He calls them 'ideas' - sensory ideas. On finding that these sensory ideas are not consciously originated by himself, he comes to think that these ideas must have some external cause or causes. He resorts to a causal inference in order to arrive finally - so he supposes - at material things as their causes.

Kant contends, as we have already noted before, that the Cartesian causal inference is untrustworthy, being inconclusive. As far as he can judge, this sort of 'precarious'[50] (inconclusive) inference serves only to render the existence of material things *doubtful.* This ultimate scepticism which came upon Descartes unawares, and is the result of his attempt to tide over his initial scepticism regarding the existence of material things, is brought under our notice clearly and for the first time by Kant, who has characterized it as a sort of idealism, namely 'empirical idealism' or 'sceptical idealism', as he has chosen to call it in the first edition of the *Critique of Pure Reason*[51] (and also in his *Prolegomena to Any Future Metaphysics*[52], published before the second edition of the *Critique).* For Kant, Descartes' final scepticism or idealism is only the consequence of his initial blunder consisting in the failure to see that material things are basically *objects of the senses* - that is, objects which are within the reach of our sensibility.

The following passage will show how Kant uses the term 'idealism' in his characterization of Descartes' final philosophical position as empirical or sceptical idealism. [The passage occurs immediately after his criticism of the Cartesian inference on the ground that it makes the existence of material things doubtful.]

> The term *'idealist*[1] is not, therefore, to be understood [here] as applying to those who deny the existence of external objects of the senses, but only to those who do not admit that their existence is known through immediate perception, and who therefore conclude that we can never, by way of any possible experience, be completely certain as to their reality.[53]

Unlike Descartes, Kant treats material things as *appearances,* in the nonpejorative sense of objects of possible experience, instead of as things in themselves. He is thus able to bring them under the purview of our sensibility, and, only in co-operation with it, of the understanding. Our sensibility has its own modes of reception of objects: pure spatial and temporal modes of receiving them; and the objects as so received are called *appearances.* What we come to know as physical objects - or material things - are, as per Kant's transcendental analysis, initially appearances (in the technical sense), which are spatio-temporally received in empirical intuition as sense-manifolds, and are further determined by the understanding through its *a priori* categorial contributions to the taken-up sense-manifolds for conceptual recognition of them as objects at all (in the strong sense of 'objects', as things having qualities, and so on), and through its articulations of them in terms of some specific and appropriate empirical concepts as this or that determinate physical object of knowledge (called a phenomenon). Leaving details apart, the point to be particularly noted is that, according to Kant, there is, in objective knowledge, a definite and undeniable role of sense: that of empirical intuition, or perception. In order to lay stress on this point, Kant, in the present context of his critique of the Cartesian account, is insisting that physical or spatial objects - external material things - are in their ways available to us as primarily *given* objects of immediate perception. He is, by advocating this view, able to avoid being an empirical idealist, that is, being eventually a sceptic, with regard to the reality of external material things.

Descartes, on the other hand, started as a *transcendental realist,* and in consequence became willy-nilly an *empirical idealist*[54]. A transcendental realist, for Kant, is a philosopher who - after wrongly assuming that the objects of our senses, in order to be *external* in the strict sense, must possess an existence in themselves quite apart from the senses - comes to find that, from his standpoint, all our sensuous representations are insufficient to guarantee their existence, and is accordingly obliged to become an *empirical idealist,* that is, virtually a sceptic as regards the reality of outer objects.

Kant, by adopting a different point of view, namely, that of *transcendental idealism,* is able, as an eventual *empirical realist,* to offer a sufficient refutation of the Cartesian scepticism as to the reality of empirically external objects. As he puts it :

> Empirical idealism, and its mistaken questionings as to the objective reality of our outer perceptions, is already sufficiently refuted, when it has been shown that outer perception yields immediate proof of something actual in space, and that this space, although in itself only a mere form of representations, has objective reality in relation to all outer appearances, which also are nothing else than mere representations [in the transcendental-idealist sense]; and when it has likewise been shown that in the absence of perception even imagining and dreaming are not possible,[55] and that our outer senses, as regards the data from which experience can arise, have therefore their actual corresponding objects in space. [A 376 - 377]

As concerns the passage quoted at the outset of 4.4.3.2: its import, which we have been so long trying to explain, will have been by now amply clear.

So this chapter may be drawn to a close at this point.

NOTES

1 E.g.–

(a) Cf. J. P. Mahaffy and J. H. Bernard, *Kant's Critical Philosophy,* First Edition 1889, Orient Publications, Delhi, First Indian Reprint 1988, Kritik of the Fourth Paralogism of Transcendental Psychology, in Appendix C (pp. 203-213); p. 204 note 1;

also

(b) See N. Kemp Smith, *A Commentary to Kant's 'Critique of Pure Reason',* Macmillan & Co. Ltd, London, 1918, pp 301ff, and pp. 308ff. ;

(c) See also A. C. Ewing, *A Short Commentary on Kant's* 'Critique of Pure Reason', Methuen & Co. Ltd, London, 1961, pp. 176ff. ;

(d) See also Jonathan Bennett, *Kant's Analytic,* Cambridge University Press, Cambridge, 1966, § 52 ('Kant's two refutations of empirical idealism'), pp. 215ff;

also

(e) See C. D. Broad, *Kant: An Introduction,* ed. C. Lewy, Cambridge University Press, Cambridge, reprinted, 1979; 4.3.4.1: Refutation A (pp. 188ff); and 4.3.4.2 Refutation B (pp. 194ff);

and so on.

2 For Kant's definition of 'idealism' in this sense in the First Edition of the *Critique,* see A 368 - 369, (Kemp Smith's translation, p. 345, 3rd para.)

3 See p. 13 above.

4 A 368 (Kemp Smith's transl. p. 345, 2nd para).

5 The inference *has got to be inconclusive,* because in this sort of inference one can never be sure of having considered the claims of all *possible* candidates for the status of the cause.

6 Kant, *loc. cit.*

7 What is *only* inferred is open to all the dangers of inference, because in such a case the inference cannot be supported by any other available canon of evidence, say, by any subsequent *perceptual* corroboration; for

the objects which are here alleged to be inferred by Descartes are not admitted by him to be in principle open to perception at all; nor are they shown by him to be of the sort to be available to us still otherwise, in case the inference is challenged.

8 Kant, *loc. cit.*

9 H. J. Paton, *Kant's Metaphysic of Experience,* volume two, George Allen & Unwin, London, 1970, LI § 4, p. 381.

10 Cf. Paul Guyer, *Kant,* Routledge, Taylor & Francis Group; First published 2006, First Indian Reprint 2008, p. 117.

11 Space, for Kant, is primarily represented immediately - i.e. intuitively. Accordingly, spatial objects - objects in space - must allow of being represented immediately (intuitively) - at least primarily.

12 Kant says : 'Space is .... the form of all appearances of outer sense. It is the .... condition .... under which alone outer intuition is possible for us'. A 26 = B 42.

13 A 373.

14 *Ibidem.*

15 *Ibidem.*

16 'Objects are *given* to us by means of sensibility, and it alone yields us *intuitions; ....'* 'But all thought must, directly or indirectly, ... relate ultimately to intuitions, and therefore, with us, to sensibility, because in no other way can an object be given to us.' [A 19]

17 On the arguments for the view that primary representation of space is an *a priori intuition,* see the Transcendental Aesthetic of the *Critique,* esp. A 23ff.

18 'Possible' here means possibility of explanation. [Kemp Smith, following Vaihinger, has in some other context distinguished and explained several meanings of the word 'possible'. See Kemp Smith's *Commentary,* pp. 43ff]

19 That by 'form' here Kant means *condition* will be clear from the passage quoted above in note 12.

20 Kant himself sometimes does so for 'convenience' sake. See, for example, Kemp Smith's translation, p. 349. fifth and sixth lines.

21 'Element' is an important Kantian expression. The first part of his *Critique of Pure Reason* is entitled *Transcendental Doctrine of Elements,* in which the a *priori* elements are isolated for a special study from the a *posteriori* ones involved in knowledge.

22 In order to be known, objects have to be given and thought, according to Kant. He says: 'the conditions under which alone the objects of human knowledge are given must precede those under which they are thought'. (A 16 = B30) He is here ascribing a sort of logical priority to *being given* over *being thought* by means of concepts in the knowledge situation: indeed, unless something is given in intuition, there is nothing to think about by conception. The Kantian emphasis on the *primacy* of intuition may serve as a check on the rationalist tendency to underestimate the role of empirical intuition in knowledge. Kant has attached no less importance, however, to conception for knowledge. His is a doctrine of co-operation, indeed, between sensible (non-intellectual) intuition and conception in knowledge.

The word 'initially', as used in our exposition, is intended to be taken only in the aforementioned sense of *primarily,* and not in such a way as to suggest that empirical intuition is *sufficient* for knowledge of spatial or corporeal objects.

23 Cf. *Critique,* A 371 (Kemp Smith's trans. p. 347, 1st para., last two lines).

24 A 376.

25 *Ibidem.*

26 A 377. Although the proof, as a proof, cannot, strictly speaking, be an *immediate* proof, Kant has called it so, because its canon of evidence is intuition, that is, as he says, 'immediate perception (consciousness)'. (A 371)

27 Ewing, *Short Commentary,* p. 176.

28 *Ibid.,* p. 177.

29 A transcendental idealist (Kant) is a dualist, because he admits the existence of both matter and mind. As is to be expected, he at A 379 qualifies this dualism as 'dualism only in the empirical sense'. It is an empirical dualism, because it is, for him, valid, only with respect to appearances or phenomena. It is not valid, that is to say, with respect to

things in themselves. As we cannot know their nature, we cannot apply to them the distinction between the material and the mental. See Kant's explicit statement to this effect at A 379 - 380. Things in themselves being unknown and unknowable, we cannot, for him, distinguish some of them as physical from the others as if they were mental. Thus a transcendental idealist can be only an empirical dualist, and not a transcendental dualist.

30 A 369.

31 A 491 = B 519.

32 At A 26 = B42 Kant says : 'It is, therefore solely from the human standpoint that we can speak of space, of extended things, etc.' For similar remarks about time, see A 35 (Kemp Smith's translation., pp. 77-78.

33 In G. Bird's words, we may here say: 'it is [for Kant] a natural inference from the status ascribed to space and time, that this status should be ascribed also to the objects, appearances, which are in them'. See Graham Bird, *Kant's Theory of Knowledge,* Routledge & Kegan Paul, London, 1962, 2nd impression 1965, p. 47.

34 A 372.

35 Sebastian Gardner, 'Kant', in *Philosophy* 2, ed. A. C. Grayling, Oxford University Press, Oxford, reprinted in paperback 2007, p. 586.

36 Bird, *loc. cit.*

37 *Ibid.,* p. 46.

38 *Ibid.,* p. 47.

39 Sec, e.g., A 378 (end) - A 379 (beginning); also B 66.

40 *Critique,* A 373.

41 I.e. in the transcendental-idealist sense.

42 Kemp Smith's translation, p. 347, towards the end of the first paragraph.

43 A34 = B 50.

44 A 33 = B 49.

45 A35 = B 51.

[46] A 34 = B 50.

[47] The expression 'dependent on our sensibility' is taken from A 378. As for the necessity which is mentioned, it is only transcendental necessity.

[48] Ewing, *Short Commentary,* p. 183.

[49] A 371 (Kemp Smith's translation, p. 347, first three lines of the 2nd para.).

[50] The term, *precarious,* is taken from Mahaffy and Bernard's translation of Kant's 'Kritik of the Fourth Paralogism of Transcendental Psychology'. See their *Kant's Critical Philosophy,* p. 204, 2nd para.

[51] *Critique:*
For the name 'empirical idealism', see e.g. A 376 (towards the end);
For the name 'sceptical idealism', see e.g. A 378 (towards the end).

[52] *Prolegomena to Any Future Metaphysics* (translated, and ed. L. W. Beck, Library of Liberal Arts, Bobbs-Merrill Co., Inc., Indianapolis, 1976):
For the name 'empirical idealism', see p. 40 (towards the end);
For the name 'sceptical idealism', see p. 125 (end of the first para.) Appendix.

[53] *Critique,* A 368-369.

[54] Cf. A 369.

[55] Thus at 373-374 Kant has already argued as follows: 'Perception exhibits the reality of something in space; and in the absence of perception no power of imagination can invent and produce that something'.

CHAPTER FIVE

KANT'S PROOF OF THE EXISTENCE OF EXTERNAL THINGS IN SPACE (AS GIVEN IN THE SECOND EDITION OF THE *CRITIQUE)*

5.1 Foreword

In the second edition of the *Critique*, Kant has given us a new[1] proof of the existence of external things, which he has called 'the existence of objects in space outside us'[2]. The proof is given in the section entitled 'Refutation of Idealism'. The word 'idealism' here refers to what he has called 'the *problematic* idealism of Descartes'[3]. Kant's second-edition proof of the existence of external spatial things and his refutation of the Cartesian problematic idealism are inseparably connected with each other. The first thing to do in this chapter is to explain how the phrase 'problematic idealism' is to be construed.

5.2 Explaining the Meaning of Kant's Phrase 'The Problematic Idealism of Descartes'

By '*problematic* idealism', Kant simply means the Cartesian scepticism. But what sort of scepticism on the part of Descartes does he mean here (at B 274-75 of the *Critique) ?* There are some eminent writers (Strawson and Copleston, to mention only two of them) who think that the Cartesian scepticism signifies the doubts which Descartes expressed in the *First Meditation* regarding the existence of external, material, things.

Thus Strawson observes :

> .... the execution of Kant's programme for a positive

> metaphysics is held to entail the rejection of what he calls 'problematic' idealism, even if such idealism is only the methodological starting-point, rather than the terminus, of philosophical reflection[4].

And Copleston, in the course of a brief examination of 'the accuracy of Kant's historical remarks', observes :

> As for Descartes, he certainly maintains that we can apply 'hyperbolical' doubt to the existence of external finite things; but he also maintained that reason can overcome this doubt . . . .[5]

Strawson's and Copleston's view, taken as an interpretation of the Kantian understanding of the Cartesian scepticism, is not, however, quite correct, as it does not fit in well with the present context. In this context, as one can indeed see by carefully reading the text, Kant is referring to Descartes' attempted inferential proof of the existence of external, material, things. We may recall that he has already observed in the first edition of the *Critique,* by a direct criticism of the Cartesian proof, that this proof is *inconclusive.* The inconclusiveness of the proof shows, according to Kant, that the proof has rather made the very existence of external material things uncertain, doubtful or problematic. It is to this uncertainty or dubiousness that Kant is referring, in the second edition, by saying by implication that the scepticism associated with the conclusion of Descartes' proof may well be described as 'the *problematic* idealism of Descartes'. 'Idealism' here stands for the position of a philosopher who, unlike Berkeley, does not deny, but doubts - that is, makes problematic - the existence of external things in space.[6]

It may be noted that Kant's direct criticism which was made at A368 of the *Critique* to expose the inconclusiveness of Descartes' merely inferential-*cum*-causal proof of the existence of external material things was - unlike his other criticisms of Descartes in the first edition - non-committal and quite theory-neutral. That is why we have not considered it inappropriate to allude to it in connection with his B-edition Refutation of the Cartesian proof. Moreover, Kant himself attaches so much importance to his direct anti-Cartesian criticism contained in the A368 passage that he is led to repeat it almost verbatim even in the second-edition 'Refutation'.[7] One has only to compare the following passage, cited from B276 with the A368 passage which is referred to above and was already quoted in the last chapter, to be able to appreciate this point :

> Idealism assumed that the only immediate experience is inner experience, and that from it we can only *infer* outer things - and this, moreover, only in an untrustworthy manner, as in all cases where we are inferring from given effects to determinate causes. In this particular case, the cause of the representations, which we ascribe, perhaps falsely, to outer things, may lie in ourselves.[8]

What we have said above in justification of our construal of the Kantian expression 'the *problematic* idealism of Descartes' will have been sufficient by now. We may pass on to make next a study of Kant's proof in the second edition.

5.3 Explaining Kant's Proof, in the Second Edition, of the Existence of External Spatial Things

Kant proceeds by stating first his *thesis* to be proved, and then by giving his *proof* of the thesis. We have to start, then, with his thesis.

5.3.1 Kant's thesis explained

The thesis in Kant's second-edition proof under consideration, as it is stated by him, may not be clear immediately. So some sort of perspective for it has to be provided first. It can be provided only by reference to Descartes' own method of procedure followed in the *Meditations.* As we all know, he has started there by claiming to have proved, first of all, the existence of himself - that is, the existence of his own mind - by appealing to a kind of direct intuition, which has come to be known as intellectual intuition. In his own mind, after proving its existence, he next finds certain ideas. Then, by making a suitable selection from among these ideas, he proceeds to prove the existence of God on the basis of the selected idea. At long last he arrives at the final chapter of the *Meditations* to offer a proof of the existence of external things in space. This is the perspective which should all along be kept in view in order to understand why and how Kant has started his second-edition proof in the way he has done.

In the second-edition 'Refutation', Kant is going to argue that the consciousness of myself - that is, of my own existence - , as determined in time, presupposes the existence of external things in space.

The *thesis* of his second-edition 'Refutation' is accordingly worded as :

> *The mere, but empirically determined, consciousness of my own existence proves the existence of objects in space outside me.*[9]

What does Kant mean by the phrase 'empirically determined consciousness of my own existence' ? As has been pointed out by Paul Guyer, the full meaning of the phrase cannot come out prior to an examination of the argument presented in Kant's proof of the thesis.[10] At present the meaning of the phrase can be only briefly indicated : thus, it means consciousness of my own existence as manifested through a succession of thoughts, ideas, etc., occurring in time. The burden of Kant's argument is that this consciousness is not possible without the existence of outer objects in space.

So we have to turn now to a study of Kant's proof of the thesis stated above.

5.3.2 Explanation of Kant's proof of the thesis

Kant's *proof* under reference 'is excessively compact and incomplete'.[11] So we are required to explain it by making use of materials from different sources - namely, 'Refutation of Idealism' (esp. B275ff), some other parts of the *Critique* (esp. '*First Analogy*', B224ff), *Preface to the Second Edition* (Bxxxix - xli, footnote), and his Reflexions[12] (which are his after-thoughts on the 'Refutation'). A comprehensive study of Kant's *proof*' is expected to give us a complete picture of his argument.

Now, in order to understand Kant's proof of the thesis mentioned above, it is necessary to appreciate what exactly he finds to be wrong in Descartes' initial proof, namely, the proof of the existence of himself. Descartes has tried to prove the existence of himself - that is, of his mind - by taking his mind in isolation. He takes the mind as such, pure and simple. He takes the *sum* in *cogito ergo sum* as a pure datum. For Kant, however, such a pure datum is not intelligible to us. For time, according to him, is the universal form of intuition. So the existence of anything, if we are to know it, must show itself in time. The self of which I am aware is, then, for him, my empirical self,[13] which has determinate locations in time. 'I am conscious of my own existence as determined in time' - Kant says.[14] 'A determinate position in time is' - as Douglas Burnham and Harvey Young put it - 'part of what we mean when we say that something really exists, rather than is imaginary.'[15] It makes no sense to say simply : 'I am'. It only makes sense to say: 'I am *in time*'. I need to be able to apply such temporal predicates as 'then', 'now', 'later', to myself.[16] I can be aware of myself through, and only through, a succession of ideas as they occur in time - that is, only through a temporal series or order of representations.

But a succession of ideas involves a *change* - namely, a change in ideas as they occur and form a temporal order of them. But change presupposes something *permanent* in perception. As Kant says: 'All determination of time presupposes something *permanent* in perception.'[17] In the present case, what can this *permanent* be ? This is Kant's point of inquiry.

In pursuing this inquiry, Kant is led to consider and exclude several alternatives till at last he comes to the alternative that the required *permanent* something is provided by an objective, law-governed, external world.

It has to be explained now how Kant excludes the various alternatives before he comes to the last one, which he accepts.

It must be mentioned here that the various alternatives examined by him are not to be found at one place, but at different places, in the *Critique.* As has already been stated before, we are required here to look beyond the argument as presented by Kant in the 'Refutation'.

The first alternative is this. It may be supposed that the required permanent something is provided by the *self* as substance. Kant rejects this alternative at once. For we have no direct apprehension, and hence no knowledge, of ourselves as substantial entities. At B277, he says :

> Certainly, the representation 'I am', which expresses the consciousness that can accompany all thought, immediately includes in itself the existence of a subject; but it does not so include any *knowledge* of the subject, ... For this we require, in addition to the thought of something existing, also [non-intellectual][18] intuition, and in this case inner intuition, in respect of which, that is, of time, the subject must be determined.[19]

The point is that all that we can know about ourselves is a

succession of our ideas occurring in time. But then we are straight back to our problem.

Another alternative which arises is this. It may be supposed that *time* itself can provide the permanent something required for the purpose. Against this alternative, there is the Kantian argument (presented in the *First Analogy*): 'Now time cannot by itself be perceived.' [B225] Time is no doubt intuited *a priori*, but time is not presentable as a fixed, visible, substantial something within which items are given along with their locations.[20] Time is intuited *a priori* only as a form of intuition - that is, along with, and not as a separably mentionable background to, what is presented empirically in it.

There is a further possibility for Kant to rule out next. May it not be that the permanent representation itself meets the requirement of permanence in the present case ? Kant, for himself, does not admit the possibility of a *permanent representation*. He admits in the Preface to the Second Edition of the *Critique* that, in so far as we think of something permanent, we have indeed the representation of something *permanent;* but he hastens to point out that this representation 'is not the same as *permanent representation*'. As he puts it: 'The representation of something *permanent* in existence is not the same as *permanent representation* '.[21] He argues that all representations are by their very nature 'transitory and variable', and that the representation of something permanent, in so far as it is a representation, is no exception to this general rule.[22]

In this way the suggestion that there *is a permanent representation* which meets the requirement of permanence in the present case is ruled out by Kant.

What, then, can be the *permanent* something in reference to which a determinate succession of ideas is possible (that is, intelligible) ?

To this the Kantian answer would be in terms of the view reached through the following argument (which is to be called the 'Refutation' - argument amplified and supplemented in the light of materials provided elsewhere) :

The required permanent something cannot be something *in me*, 'since it is only through this permanent that my existence in time can itself be determined'.[23] As it cannot be something existing in me, it must be, therefore, something existing *outside me*. The permanent something which is required to be outside me must be 'a *thing* outside me and not . . . . the mere *representation* of a thing outside me'.[24] The reason why this distinction is made needs perhaps some clarification, and the clarification is to be found in a footnote to the Preface to the Second Edition (see esp. Bxli part of the footnote) :

The *representation* of a thing outside me is a representation, and is, as such, 'transitory and variable'; so it cannot provide anything permanent. That is why it has been said that the required permanent something outside me must be a *thing* outside me, and not merely the *representation* of a thing outside me.

It follows from what has been said so far that the determination of my existence in time (through the succession of my ideas) is possible only through the actual existence of things outside me.[25]

In one of his after-thoughts on the 'Refutation', Kant expressly brings *space* into the argument. He writes: Space 'cannot represent that which is in us', but 'really signifies . . . . a relation to a real thing outside us' [*R* 6317, 18 : 627-8][26]. This is indeed reminiscent of 'Transcendental Aesthetic'. Space is a form of *outer* intuition, and as such is that through which alone we represent things outside us. Things outside us are accordingly outside us *in space.* [Kant's use of the expression 'in space' in the *Thesis* of his 'Refutation of Idealism' is hereby explained.]

It is in the above way that Kant has sought to prove that the determinate consciousness of my own existence (that is, of the existence of my empirical self through a succession of my ideas) requires for its possibility 'the existence of objects in space outside me'.

In the final analysis, Kant's argument, as explained above, boils down to this: we can assign a determinate temporal order to our ideas (representations), and in this way come to attain the consciousness of self-existence, by interpreting them as representations of an objective, law-governed, external world. The spatial objects of the external world are considered to be relatively stable, persistent, objects[27] which can fulfil the requirement of permanence in the case under consideration.

The impression must not be had that, in Kant's view, permanence is something discovered there outside us[28]. Rather it is, for him, presupposed *a priori* according to the category of substance, and then *found in* material objects, in so far as these are represented in the knowledge situation through the category of substance.[29]

To obviate misunderstanding, Kant ends up his second-edition proof of the existence of external material things with this remark:

Because the existence of external things is required for a determinate consciousness of the self, it is not to be supposed that every intuitive representation of an external thing involves at the same time the existence of that thing; for such a representation may well be due to mere imagination (as in an illusion or delusion or dream)'[30]. All that the 'Refutation' has sought to show 'is that inner experience in general is possible only through outer experience in general'.[31] Whether a particular 'supposed experience' is, or is not, purely imaginary has to be decided on the merits of the case, and in accordance with 'the criteria of all real experience'.[32]

5.4 Observations on Certain Other Points

The following observations may be of some use.

(a) On the untenability of Prichard's interpretation of Kant's second-edition proof of the existence of external things

H. A. Prichard in his book, *Kant's Theory of Knowledge*, maintains that Kant in the second-edition 'Refutation' seeks to prove just the existence of things in themselves. Referring to Kant's distinction between 'a *thing* outside me' and 'the mere *representation* of a thing outside me', Prichard argues that a thing outside me, as distinguished from a mere representation of it, has to be, in Kant's philosophy, a thing in itself. As he (Prichard) puts it :

> The phrase must . . . ., primarily, mean a thing external to, in the sense of independent of, my mind, i.e. a thing in itself.[33]

Prichard's interpretation is nowadays generally discarded,[34] and does not, therefore, call for an elaborate discussion. The principal objections to this interpretation are, as pointed out by Ewing,[35] the following two :

First, things outside me are here referred to by Kant as 'objects in space'. Objects in space are not, for him, things in themselves.[36]

Secondly, Kant's argument in the 'Refutation' depends in part on his argument in the *First Analogy*, which admittedly refers to only phenomena.

(b) On the main difference between Kant's first-edition and second-edition proofs of the existence of material things

It is needful to point out the main difference between Kant's arguments in the two editions for the existence of material things. It is this :

In the first edition Kant has argued that material things allow of being perceived immediately in space and time, which are, though transcendentally ideal, also empirically real, and that, therefore, there is no need to resort to any precarious inference in order to prove their existence.[37] In the second edition Kant has presented a stronger argument. He has shown that the existence of spatial things outside me is already presupposed in my determinate self-consciousness through a succession of my ideas, and therefore *cannot* be inferred from my ideas (non-fallaciously, i.e. without the fallacy of circularity).

(c) A brief comparison of Kant's second-edition proof with Descartes' proof of the existence of external things in space

Looking back at Descartes in the end, we see that he has assigned a kind of priority to inner experience over the outer. He starts with the inner consciousness, and tries to come out of it and reach out to the outer world of corporeal objects on the basis of an untrustworthy inference. Kant in his 'Refutation of Idealism' has clearly shown that the Cartesian priority is rnisplaced. He has shown that if we are to be internally conscious of ourselves, or of anything at all, as determined in time, this consciousness must be conditioned by the existence of real things in space outside us. Even our representation of the mere products of imagination (as in dreams and delusions) is, for Kant, 'the reproduction of previous outer perceptions, which . . . . are possible only through the reality of outer objects'.[38] This is at once his proof of the actual existence of outer things generally and his disproof of the Cartesian view that it is the inner which has a priority over the outer.

NOTES

1 See *Critique of Pure Reason,* Kemp Smith's translation., p.34 n., Kant refers to his second-edition 'Refutation' as 'the new refutation'.

2 B275. see 'Refutation of Idealism': *Thesis.*

3 B274.

4 P.F. Strawson, *The Bounds of Sense,* Methuen, London, 1966, p. 19.

5 F. Copleston, S.J. *A History of Philosophy,* vol. VI *{Modern Philosophy: From the French Enlightenment to Kant),* Doubleday, New York, Image edition, 1994, p. 273.

6 B274.

7 That there is 'a passage occurring in both editions' of the *Critique* (in connection with the 'Refutation of Idealism') is an important consideration, according to J. Bennett; cf his *Kant's Analytic,* Cambridge University Press, 1966, p. 216.
[This is written because there is a controversy among Kant-scholars on the question whether Kant's first-edition refutation is totally suppressed in the second-edition.]

8 Kemp Smith's translation., p. 245 (towards the end).

9 B275.

10 Cf. Paul Guyer, *Kant,* Routledge, London, First Indian reprint 2008, p. 118, 2nd para.

11 *Ibid.,* p. 117.

12 *Reflexionen* (containing Kant's marginal notes, volumes 14-20 and 23 of the Academy edition). As there is no English translation of the work, we have to depend on Guyer's extracts from this work in his own translation.

13 Cf. Copleston, *op. cit.,* p. 273 note 1.

14 *Critique,* B275.

15 Douglas Burnham and Harvey Young, *Kant's 'Critique of Pure Reason',* Edinburgh University Press, Edinburgh, 2007, pp. 127f.

16 *Ibid., p. 127.*

17 B275.

[18] According to Kant, all *our* (i.e. humanly possible) intuitions are sensible, that is, non-intellectual. He says: 'now, as the Aesthetic has shown, the only intuition possible to us is sensible . . . .' (B146). 'Sensible intuition is either pure intuition . . . . or empirical intuition . . . .' (B147)

[19] Kemp Smith's translation., p. 246 (first para.).

[20] Cf. Burnham and Young, *op. cit.*, p. 128.

[21] B-Preface, footnote continuing on Bxli. Kemp Smith's translation., p. 36 n.

[22] *Ibidem.*

[23] B275.

[24] *Ibidem.*

[25] This is Kant's own conclusion in the *'Proof* in the *'Refutation* : see B275-276.

[26] Cited and translated by Guyer, *op. cit.*, p. 120.

[27] Cf. Strawson, *op. cit.*, pp. 125ff, also p. 27.

[28] Thus Kant says: 'permanence is not obtained from outer experience, but is presupposed *a priori* . . . .' B278.

[29] Burnham and Young, *op.cit.*, pp. 128-129.

[30] *Critique*, B278.

[31] B 278-279.

[32] B279.

[33] H. A. Prichard, *Kant's Theory of Knowledge*, Clarendon, Oxford, 1909, p. 322.

[34] See A. C. Ewing, *A Short Commentary on Kant's 'Critique of Pure Reason'*, 1961, p. 178; Cf. also Paton, *Kant's Metaphysic of Experience*, vol. two, p. 378, and note 3 on the same page.

[35] Ewing, *loc. cit.*

[36] For discussion of Kant's view that space does not represent any property of things in themselves, see, however, Charles Parsons, 'The Transcendental Aesthetic', esp. section IV, in Paul Guyer, ed., *The*

Cambridge Companion to Kant, Cambridge University Press, Cambridge, reprinted 1999, pp. 62-100 (esp. pp. 80ff).

[37] On the point that no inference is here needed, consult also the following statement made by Kant at A371 :
'In order to arrive at the reality of outer objects I have just as little need to resort to inference as I have in regard to the reality of the object of my inner sense, that is, in regard to the reality of my thoughts. [Kemp Smith's translation., p. 347]

[38] B278 (Kemp Smith's translation, p. 247).

CHAPTER SIX

AN EXAMINATION OF KANT'S 'PROOFS' IN THE TWO EDITIONS OF THE CRITIQUE

6.1 Foreword

Kant's proofs of the existence of external things in space, as given in the two editions of the *Critique of Pure Reason,* are open to objections, of which the chief ones are taken up and examined in the present chapter.

Kant's omission of the first-edition proof of the existence of external spatial things from the second-edition of the *Critique* need not be taken to signify that he has thought his earlier view to be *false,* but might have been due to some other considerations. His second-edition 'proof', bearing the title 'Refutation of Idealism', has been entered quite unexpectedly into a place much earlier than the place where the Fourth Paralogism (A) containing his first-edition 'proof' was treated previously. So there appears to be some truth in J. P. Mahaffy's observation with regard to the Fourth Paralogism (A) : 'This paralogism does not appear in the Second Edition probably because the "Refutation" had already settled the question as to the relative dignity and priority of the internal and external experience'.[1]

Anyway, we should attach as much importance to Kant's first-edition 'proof as is generally attached to the second-edition 'proof', even though the former has been expunged by him from the second-edition. We have already given a statement of the first-edition 'proof', and should not now abstain from evaluating it. Even in the second-edition 'proof' much is presupposed which comes from acquiescence in the doctrine of transcendental idealism - a doctrine which is the basis of the first-edition 'proof'.

6.2 A Critical Appraisal of Kant's First-Edition 'Proof'

We may begin with the standard objection to the first-edition 'proof'.

6.2.1 The charge of Berkeleyan subjectivism against Kant examined

In the course of his treatment of the Fourth Paralogism (A), Kant has made some striking observations, which, taken out of their context and interpreted carelessly, are very misleading. Thus, he has said that matter is 'only a species of representations (intuition)' - that 'External objects (bodies), however, are mere appearances, and are therefore nothing but a species of my representations', and so on.[2] Again, he has said that 'space itself is in us'[3], and has sometimes argued that material things (bodies), in so far as they are given in space, are in us, because space itself is in us.[4] He means that material things in respect of their purely spatial characteristics are in us. And the implication of this observation, which is clearly drawn by him at one point, is this : that just as we are immediately certain of the reality of our thoughts or ideas which are in us, so also we are immediately certain of the reality or actuality of space and spatial objects which are in us.[5]

These and such observations on the part of Kant led some of his contemporaries (notably C. Garve) to bring against him the charge of subjectivism or Berkeleyanism (Berkeleianism) immediately after publication of the first-edition of the *Critique.*[6] Even some eminent, more modern, writers like Strawson have repeated this charge. Thus Strawson has observed : 'Kant, as transcendental idealist, is closer to Berkeley than he acknowledges.'[7] It is not, however, difficult to show that the charge of Berkeleyan subjectivism brought against Kant is a mistaken charge.

Physical objects are objects *in* space. Now, the view that space is *in us* is formulated by Kant from the point of view of his *transcendental idealism,* which is different from Berkeley's *empirical idealism.* Berkeley has sought to explain the ideas of space, and of objects in space, in terms of certain appropriate sensations. In his *Essay towards a New Theory of Vision* (1709), Berkeley seeks to explain our original idea of space, in its three dimensions of length, breadth, and thickness, in terms of sensations of contact, muscular resistance, and locomotive effort.[8] A. C. Fraser explains this Berkeleyan view by observing that if we never experienced locomotive sensations, we could not understand what the word 'space' means; 'for it means *room to move in,* - an idea we could not have had without experience of movement.'[9] We thus see that Kant has correctly stated Berkeley's view by saying in the *Prolegomena* in the course of making a reply to his contemporary's charge of Berkeleyanism against him that

> Berkeley .... regarded space as a mere empirical representation that, like the appearance it contains, is, together with its determinations, known to us only by means of experience or perception.[10]

As for Kant himself, he holds, on the contrary, that space is an object of *a priori* intuition.[11] And from this view, taken in conjunction with some further considerations, he derives ultimately the view that space is *transcendentally ideal.*[12] The doctrine of the transcendental ideality of space is one of the main pillars on which his doctrine of transcendental idealism hinges. Under Kant's idealism, then, there is an *a priori* foundation. Surely, this cannot be said with regard to Berkeley's idealism. Kant points out in the *Prolegomena* that

> as truth rests on universal and necessary laws as its criteria, experience, according to Berkeley, can have no criteria of truth because its phenomena (according to him)[13] have nothing *a priori* at their foundation, ...[14]

This is how Kant has distinguished his own position from that of Berkeley in the *Prolegomena* in his reply to the charge of Berkeleyanism.

In his *Treatise Concerning the Principles of Human Knowledge* (1710), Berkeley has analysed our perceptions of physical objects in terms of sensations. Thus, he has argued that when we perceive what is ordinarily called a *thing,* we get sensations of various kinds, and find nothing more. He observes:

> And as several of these [sensations] are observed to accompany each other, they come to be marked by one name, and so to be reputed as one THING. Thus, for example, a certain colour, taste, smell, figure and consistence having been observed to go together, are accounted one distinct thing signified by the name *apple;* other collections of ideas *['ideas* actually imprinted on the senses', i.e. sensations][15] constitute a stone, a tree, a book, and the like sensible thing . . . .[16]

Clearly, a physical object - a thing - is, according to Berkeley, completely reducible, without remainder, to a group of sensations. Now, sensations are, for him, *in us;* and this entails, in his view, the conclusion that physical objects, as groups of sensations, are ultimately *in us.*

This Berkeleyan sort of reductionist analysis can, however, by no means be extended to Kant. [This sort of reductionist analysis is nowadays generally known as the phenomenalist analysis. Phenomenalism is a position according to which physical objects are constructions out of, and so reducible to, sense-experiences. In more sophisticated language : according to it, statements about physical objects are fully translatable into corresponding statements about sensa. The phenomenalist interpretation of Kant is called by Sebastian Gardner the 'standard picture'.[17] We are going to show in the next paragraph that the Berkeleyan sort of reductionist analysis, or its sophisticated more modern counterpart - the phenomenalist analysis - cannot be extended to the Kantian view.]

Physical objects, as objects *in* space, are not, for Kant, reducible to mere groups of sensations (sensa). He has many reasons for holding this view. One main reason is that, for him, the idea of space is not explicable at all in terms of sensations; for 'in order that certain sensations be referred to something outside me . . . ., the representation of space must be presupposed.'[18] So he regards the idea of space as an *a priori* one. Again, space, for him, is an intuition, i.e. an intuitum or intuitable.[19] The view that space is an intuition can be expressed in comparatively modem terminology by saying, as Richard Aquila points out, that space is the referent of a singular-referring expression.[20] In more sophisticated modern terminology, Kant's view that space is an intuition can be expressed by saying that the word 'space', being a singular-referring expression, cannot be eliminated in favour of any word or expression which does not refer to space. It is clear from the above considerations that, for Kant, since space is not reducible to anything else, physical objects, as objects *in* space, are not reducible to anything else.[21]

To gather the threads of discussion and come to a conclusion on the point we have been considering : Berkeley has tried to reduce a physical object to a group of sensations, and come to hold that such an object is *in us* on the ground that sensations are for him in us. But Kant as an anti-reductionist[22] cannot and does not admit the possibility of the Berkeleyan sort of reduction. So even if he (Kant) regards physical objects, or objects *in* space, as *in us* in some sense, it is clear that he does not regard them as *in us* at least in the Berkeleyan subjectivist (that is, mentalistic) sense. He says : 'With the sole exception of space there is no subjective representation, referring to something *outer,* which could be entitled [at once] objective [and] *a priori*',[23] For him, the transcendental *ideality* of space (and therewith of objects *in* space)[24] cannot be compared to the Berkeleyan sort of non-formal (and hence material) *subjectivity* of the data of the senses. Accordingly, the charge of Berkeleyan subjectivism brought against Kant's first-edition proof under reference is not well-founded.

Kant's first-edition 'proof' is also liable to other objections to which we may turn next.

6.2.2 A brief defence of transcendental idealism

It has been seen in Chapter Four that Kant's first-edition 'proof' is based on his doctrine of transcendental idealism, which in its turn depends on making a distinction between appearances and things in themselves. Ultimately, therefore, this distinction becomes all-important here. There are many who are led to reject Kant's transcendental idealism, because they cannot accept his distinction in question. Strawson is one such philosopher, and it is with his main objections to this Kantian distinction that we shall be concerned in this subsection. We may state once more that Kant's first-edition 'proof' under consideration stands or falls with his doctrine of transcendental idealism on which this 'proof' is based.

Strawson in his book *The Bounds of Sense* distinguishes between 'two strands' in Kant's thought in the *Critique of Pure Reason.*[25] These two strands are called by Strawson (i) the 'analytic' strand consisting in a set of ideas forming our conceptual scheme in terms of which we try to make the world and the experience of the world intelligible to ourselves, and (ii) the strand signified by the metaphysical doctrine of transcendental idealism, which is called metaphysical because it involves the ontological distinction between appearance and reality.[26] Strawson maintains that it is only the analytic strand of thought in the *Critique* which is worth preserving, while the doctrine of transcendental idealism has to be totally rejected, as being incoherent[27] and based on distortions[28] of the familiar notion of the appearance-reality distinction.

Strawson interprets transcendental idealism as positing a realm or 'sphere' 'of supersensible reality, of things, neither spatial nor temporal, as they are in themselves',[29]. These things are involved in a peculiar 'quasi-causal relation' of affection (which he calls, for brevity, 'the A-relation').[30] Strawson contends that this notion of affection is nonsensical (devoid of significance), judged in the light of Kant's own 'principle of significance', if applied with respect to the posited supersensible reality (the thing in itself).[31] Strawson argues that the Kantian transcendental-idealist model is a 'distortion' or 'perversion' of a familiar appearance-reality distinction made in ordinary life, and also found in a scientifically minded philosopher like Locke, for example.[32] This latter model is a model based upon shared spatio-temporal frameworks and cognitive standards, in which reality is only 'the corrected view' of appearance,[33] and in which therefore there is no radical dualism of - no ontological distinction in type between - appearance and reality.

Strawson, in his above interpretation of Kant, is committed to what is known as a 'two-object' or 'two-world' interpretation of transcendental idealism, according to which there is a realm of things (called things in themselves), neither spatial nor temporal, as numerically different from a realm of objects which are spatial and temporal objects of our (i.e. human) experience and called appearances, or rather, phenomena.[34] Opposed to it, there is another interpretation of Kant's transcendental idealism which is advocated and defended by a good many commentators, namely,

Henry Allison,[35] H. E. Matthews,[36] Ralf Meerbote,[37] and others.[38] The latter interpretation is known as the 'two-aspect' or 'two-standpoint' or 'two-conception' interpretation of Kant's contrast between appearances and things in themselves, and, therefore, of his transcendental idealism.[39]

Upon this interpretation, space and time are, for Kant, only man's 'epistemic conditions' of intuition, and so also of man's objective knowledge, of anything, and, after showing this, Kant introduces two *standpoints* about, two *conceptions* (or rather, *views)* of, things : one in which these epistemic conditions are included, and which is the view of things as they are known and knowable to us (that is, the view of things as appearances in the technical sense of objects of possible experience to us), and another from which these epistemic conditions are omitted and which is the view of *these very same things* as things as they are in themselves (that is, the transcendent view of things). On this interpretation, transcendental idealism is not at all an ontological or metaphysical theory, but rather an epistemological or methodological position. Matthews has argued to show that Kant was making, not an *ontological* point about the types of things there are, but only an *epistemological* point about the limits of human knowledge.[40]

The 'two-aspect' or the 'two-standpoint' interpretation of transcendental idealism fits in well with most of what Kant has said, and can alone make sense of his claim in the Preface to the Second Edition of the *Critique* that,

> the object is to be taken *in a twofold sense,* namely, as appearance and as thing in itself . . . .[41]
>
> [Italics in the text]

Moreover, this interpretation has a number of advantages. Thus, the distinction between the thing as appearance and the thing as it is in itself is, if taken in a *two-aspect* way, simply a necessary procedure of transcendental reflection when we seek to avoid the difficulties to which the transcendental realist view of things gives rise.[42] This distinction, understood in the light of the *two-standpoint* interpretation, enables us to avoid the Strawsonian objections.[43]

The element of 'strangeness' which Strawson finds in transcendental idealism[44] vanishes as soon as his 'two-world' interpretation of it is abandoned, and the 'two-standpoint' interpretation is adopted. Strawson objects that Kant's use of personal pronouns, such as 'we', 'our', and the like, does not refer to human beings existing in space and time, but to supersensible timeless subjects, and therefore does nothing to make any connection between the supersensible world of objects and the world of human beings.[45] In reply to this objection it may be said that, on the two-standpoint interpretation, there is no need for Kant to make any such connection, because he has not asserted the existence of any world other than the world of human beings. Matthews observes :

> Talking about human beings as timeless subjects and talking about them as temporal objects (beings which have a history, as Strawson puts it) is not talking about two worlds; it is talking about the one world in two different ways, from two different standpoints.[46]

Another severe criticism made by Strawson is that the Kantian distinction between appearances and things in themselves does not involve a significant application, but rather a distortion or perversion, of the familiar distinction between appearance and reality.[47] Our ordinary way of making this distinction is based on a shared spatial-temporal framework by making use of the concepts of identity of reference and of the corrected view; and these requirments are not fulfilled in the Kantian distinction in question. To this criticism, the following reply has been suggested by Matthews :

> It is, indeed, true - and Kant would presumably agree - that he does not use terms like 'appearance' and 'reality' in accordance with their ordinary usage. He maintains that all human experience is of 'appearances', and means that all our experience is of external objects if they appear - i.e. are represented - in their space-time relations, and of inner objects if they appear - i.e. are represented - in only their time relations. The word 'appearances' in this Kantian sense signifies spatio-temporal, and sometimes merely temporal, objects which are or can be experienced by human beings. The word 'appearances' in this Kantian sense is different from the word in its ordinary sense. [In the ordinary sense, the word stands for items which are negated, or at least modified, by a subsequent corrective judgment of experience.] But if it is granted that Kant is using the word in a way different from the ordinary way, it is quite unfair to object on the ground that he cannot give it signifance in the way that one can give significance to the word as ordinarily used.

Matthews observes :

> It does not seem to me, at least, that it is unintelligible to say that all human experience is of 'appearances' in Kant's sense; which is not necessarily to say that other beings might have a more *correct* view of things than human beings do, but simply to emphasize that the human point of view is just the *human* point of view.[48]

A connected criticism made by Strawson is that, in talking about things in themselves, Kant has violated his own 'principle of significance'. Strawson states this principle as 'the principle that we can make no significant use of concepts in propositions claiming to express knowledge unless we have empirical criteria for the application of those concepts.'[49] This means that a judgment has cognitive content only if the concepts used in it can be 'schematized', that is, can be applied to a spatio-temporal manifold. This being so, Strawson contends, no cognitively significant judgments could be made by Kant about things in themselves. Things in themselves are non-spatial and non-temporal, and, therefore, no schematized concepts could be given any application to them. The implication of the point is, according to Strawson, that Kant, in making judgments about things in themselves, violates his own principle of significance, and that, accordingly, this brings a sort of internal incoherence into the Kantian position. In reply to this objection, the first thing to be noted is that the so-called Kantian principle of significance is different from the positivists' verification principle, and that there is nothing in this Kantian principle itself to show that no judgment about things which we cannot experience has any meaning. The principle only suggests that the judgment can have no factual or empirical significance; it does not suggest, however, that the judgment has no other kind of significance, say, 'regulative', or practical, or even logical, significance. Matthews comments :

> Nor is Kant committed to saying that a judgement which is 'meaningless' in the sense of lacking factual . . . content is also 'meaningless' in the sense of 'logically absurd'. Thus, nothing prevents him saying that the experience of a being with intellectual intuition is conceivable, in the sense that it is not self-contradictory to say 'There is a being who experiences things without being affected by them', while still maintaining that such a statement can have no factual content for us. Strawson, in his comments on these remarks of Kant, seems to me to confuse these two points. The concept of a non-sensory experience is not one that we can give any application to, but this is surely not the same as saying that it is

'inconceivable' in the sense that it is an incoherent concept.[50]

Strawson's objections to transcendental idealism on the grounds that this doctrine is incoherent and unintelligible have been examined above, and found to be not strong enough. On the basis of those, and kindred, objections, it would be quite wrong, therefore, to conclude that this doctrine must be rejected. The Strawsonian objections themselves are based on an interpretation which need not be accepted.

Strawson has made another claim, however. It has already been pointed out before that there are, for him, two quite distinct, and even separable, strands of thought in the *Critique of Pure Reason*: the 'analytic' strand, and what he has called 'the metaphysics of transcendental idealism'. It is his claim that the 'analytic' strand of thought in the *Critique* is alone what is worth preserving, and that it consists in Kant's employment of what has come to be well known as 'transcendental arguments'.[51] The question is : Has transcendental argumentation the independent potential which is claimed for it by Strawson and others ? To this question the answer cannot be in the affirmative. The standard objection to transcendental arguments is that, without some tacit idealist or verificationist assumptions, such arguments yield at most conclusions about what we must think, not about how things must be, and that, therefore, such arguments fail to answer scepticism.[52]

So long we have been engaged on defending the doctrine of transcendental idealism. To return now to Kant's proof, in the first edition, of the existence of external things in space. The proof, as seen before, depends on transcendental idealism, the defence of which has served to show that the proof also has in its way some considerable strength.

It remains to undertake next a critical appraisal of Kant's

second-edition 'proof', which is contained in his second-edition 'Refutation of Idealism.'

6.3 A Critical Appraisal of Kant's Second-edition 'Proof'

In the second edition of the *Critique* Kant has tried to rebut the Cartesian sort of scepticism regarding the existence of external spatial things. His attempted proof of their existence is intended to refute scepticism by showing that 'even our inner experience, which for Descartes is indubitable, is possible only on the assumption [i.e. presupposition] of outer experience',[53] obviating any problematic inference from inner to outer experience.

How far Kant has succeeded in refuting scepticism of the Cartesian sort has, then, to be examined first.

6.3.1 How far is Kant successful in refuting the Cartesian scepticism ?

Kant's argument in his 'Refutation of Idealism' has proceeded upon the principle that if we accept one thing then we must also accept something else.[54] Thus, he has argued that if I accept the existence of myself as determined in and through the succession of my representations or ideas, then I have already accepted the existence of things outside me in space; for the latter is presupposed in the former. As he puts it in *Reflexion* 5653, 18 : 306 : 'The consciousness of other things as outside me . . . . must also be presupposed.'[55] The implication of this argument is clear enough, namely, that the existence of external things in space need not be *inferred* over again subsequently from any representations or ideas in my mind. It would be idle to pretend that we would have determinate knowledge of the order of our own representations without any presuppositions, and *only then* infer from those representations that there are external things in space. Rather it is the case that unless we assume (i.e. presuppose) that there are external things in space, we shall not have any determinate knowledge of the order of our own representations to begin with - we shall 'have only imagined orders for them, which we can just as easily imagine being otherwise.'[56]

Clearly, the above argument is a *sufficient* refutation of the Cartesian sort of scepticism.

It must be admitted, however, that the above argument does not answer scepticism of the extreme sort. For a sceptic of the extreme sort is a person who doubts even whether he can know the temporal order of his own representations, even whether he had any representations at all some minutes or some seconds ago. To a person of this sort, Paul Guyer says : '. . . . of course, you would have to be crazy to doubt *that*'.[57] Guyer continues : 'as even Descartes recognized, we cannot expect to prove anything to a lunatic - lunacy can be defined in part at least as the inability to be persuaded by a sound argument'.[58] As far as we are concerned, we see that an extreme sceptic cannot be expected to accept the principle upon which Kant's argument in the 'Refutation' has proceeded, namely, that if we accept one thing then we must also accept something else. A sceptic of the extreme sort accepts nothing (so at least he himself thinks), and therefore does not accept anything at all to begin with. But this sort of scepticism is a self-stultifying position : a man who accepts nothing does at least accept something, namely, that he accepts nothing. A sceptic of this sort needs no answer. It does not matter, therefore, if Kant's argument contains no answer to the extreme form of scepticism.

As to the Cartesian sort of scepticism (the nature of which we have already explained before) : Kant's argument in question does contain, as seen above, a sufficient refutation of it.

It remains to undertake now Richard Schacht's criticism of Kant's 'Refutation of Idealism'.

6.3.2 An examination of Richard Schacht's criticism of Kant's 'Refutation of Idealism'

Richard Schacht has criticized Kant's 'Refutation' on the ground that it has failed to refute idealism. He writes :

> Does it follow from any of this [i.e. from any step or steps in Kant's argument in the 'Refutation'] . . . that idealism is refuted ? It does only if idealism is taken simply to be the view that objects do not exist in space. This may be what some idealists have held. But if one holds, on the one hand, that objects of possible experience are spatially ordered, and on the other, that these objects of possible experiences are simply appearances, and that space in general is simply a form of human sensibility (as Kant does), does it follow that anything exists independently of *the mind,* if the mind is construed not simply as my explicit self-consciousness, but rather as that subject to which all these appearances appear, and which structures them in accordance with the forms of sensibility and the categories of the understanding ? Kant himself is not an idealist, because he contends that there must be things in themselves which underlie these appearances, and which are distinct from the mind in this broader sense. But in order really to refute idealism, he would have to be able to prove that *this* is the case; and this is something it is doubtful he can do. At any rate, he does not do it here.[59]

To this objection the following reply may be made :

Kant's 'Refutation of Idealism' is, in intention, a refutation of the Cartesian, problematic, idealism, and not of idealism *as such.* He is himself an idealist of a kind, namely, a transcendental idealist. Transcendental idealism is, for him, compatible with empirical realism, and, as has been suggested by Paton,[60] Kant has taken his stand on empirical realism when he carries out his refutation of the Cartesian, problematic or sceptical, idealism.

Schacht's criticism constitutes, therefore, a case of arguing beside the point. He has talked as if Kant in the 'Refutation' had for his objective the task of refuting idealism *in general.* To talk that way is to be guilty, indeed, of an *ignoratio elenchi.*

6.4 Final Observations on Kant's Two Proofs under Consideration

The available major objections to Kant's proofs of the existence of external things in space have been examined and found untenable. There are, then, no good reasons why it may not be admitted that his proofs in question are tolerably satisfactory. Of the two proofs, the one in the second-edition is the proof about which particularly he claims that it is 'a strict (also, as I believe, the only possible) proof of the objective reality of outer intuition.'[61] Leaving aside his personal belief that it is the only possible proof, it has to be seen whether or not it is a strict proof, as it is claimed to be, and whether or not more can be said about it.

It is noteworthy that the second-edition 'proof' has been presented by Kant in a more systematic, methodical, way than the first-edition one, by stating its *thesis,* and indicating the part called *proof* of the thesis and also the part containing his special *notes,* i.e. remarks, on some miscellaneous related points. The *proof*-part consists of certain steps of which the last one, serving as the conclusion, is grounded on the preceding ones. Ample evidence for each of the premise - like steps has been provided at the appropriate preceding places in the *Critique.* Further refinements, where he has considered them necessary, have been effected, and clarifications added, in a famous footnote to the Preface to the Second Edition. [We have also obtained further clarifications on some points from his relevant *Reflexionen.*]

The second-edition 'proof' is, for Kant, a *strict* (i.e. rigorous) *proof,* because the premises and the conclusion in the *proof*-part of it are clearly stated by him, and are evidently distinct from one another, and the conclusion is non-fallaciously arrived at from the premises.

And of the *truth* of the premises Kant has sufficiently persuaded himself and his perceptive readers by his various arguments presented in the Transcendental Aesthetic and in the relevant preceding sections in the Transcendental Analytic. He has said this, by implication, by means of his observations at Bxxxvii - Bxxxviii (Kemp Smith's translation, pp. 33-34). Consider particularly the following sentence which expresses his confidence:

> In the propositions themselves and their proofs, and also in the form and completeness of the [architectonic] plan, I have found nothing to alter. [Bxxxvii]

Kant's second-edition 'proof' of the existence of external spatial things is a strict proof, because the proof is conclusive, and it allows of being *judged* to be conclusive. And, moreover, its premises are true, and no pains have been spared *to make it clear* that they are true. It is, then, a conclusive and good proof.

As regards his first-edition 'proof', Kant has hinted (towards the end of Bxxxviii) that only 'false interpretation' is responsible for certain charges (say, on the score of Berkeleyanism in particular and phenomenalistic reductionism in general) against it. In our exposition we have tried to guard against false interpretations, as far as practicable.

Kant's second-edition 'proof' is, however, better, because it is not only more systematic, but also more relevant to the refutation of sceptical *idealism,* since it has been presented from the standpoint of empirical *realism* (even although empirical realism, for Kant, is not ultimately incompatible with transcendental idealism). From the standpoint of empirical *realism,* the much-wanted distinction between *things* and *representations* of things can easily be drawn, and has in fact been explicitly drawn by Kant himself in the *proof*-part of his second-edition proof of the existence of external things in space, as we have seen.

Accordingly, if we are required to choose between the two 'proofs' presented by Kant, our preference should be, and is here, indicated in favour of the second-edition 'proof'.

NOTES

1 J. P. Mahaffy and J. H. Bernard, *Kant's Critical Philosophy,* Delhi, First Indian Reprint 1988, p. 203 n.I. [The note is inserted by Mahaffy.]

2 *Critique,* A 370-371.

3 A370.

4 A372f.

5 Cf. A371.

6 This charge was made in the first review of the *Critique* in the *Göttingen* journal of January 19, 1782; see Kant, *Prolegomena,* trans, and ed. L. W. Beck, Indianapolis, 1976, p. 121. For a translation of the review by Christian Garve, see Brigitte Sassen, ed., *Kant's Early Critics : The Empiricist Critique of the Theoretical Philosophy,* Cambridge University Press, Cambridge, 2000.

7 P. F. Strawson, *The Bounds of Sense,* Methuen, London, 1968, p. 22.

8 On Berkeley, 'A New Theory of Vision', see A. C. Fraser, ed., *Selections from Berkeley,* Annotated, Clarendon, Oxford, 1910, pp. 175-219.

9 *Ibid.,* Prefatory Note, p. 171.

10 Kant, *Prolegomena,* Appendix, Beck's translation., p. 124.

11 *Critique,* A23-25, B38-40.

12 A26-28 = B42-44.

13 On Berkeley's use of the term, see Fraser, *op. cit.,* p. 32 n.1.

14 *Prolegomena;* Beck, *loc. cit.*

15 Berkeley, 'Principles', II, 1, in Fraser's edition, p. 32.

16 *Ibid.,* pp. 32-33.

17 Sebastian Gardner, 'Kant', in A. C. Grayling, ed., *Philosophy 2,* Oxford University Press, reprinted in 2007, p. 603.

18 *Critique,* A23 = B38.

19 See C. D. Broad, *Kant : An Introduction,* Cambridge University Press, Cambridge, reprinted 1979, p. 31.

[20] Richard Aquila, 'Concepts, Objects and the Analytic in Kant', in L.W. Beck, ed., *Proceedings of the Third International Kant Congress,* (1970), D. Reidel, Dordrecht - Holland, 1972, p. 215.

[21] *Vide ibidem.*

[22] The term 'anti-reductionist', in its application to Kant, is borrowed from G. G. Brittan, Jr. For his treatment of Kant's anti-reductionism in its different aspects, see his book, *Kant's Theory of Science,* Princeton University Press, Princeton, New Jersey, 1978, esp. ch. I.

[23] *Critique,* A28 = B44.

[24] Cf. *Critique,* B66 (Kemp Smith's transl., p. 87, second para., second line).

[25] Strawson, *op. cit.,* p. 16 and *passim.*

[26] That the Kantian distinction between appearance and reality (that is, a thing in itself) is *ontological* is a view held by Strawson, and no doubt by some others, but certainly not by all commentators. We follow Allison and Matthews and others in avoiding this view in this work, as will be clear before long.

[27] Strawson, *op. cit.,* p. 16 and *passim.*

[28] *Ibid.,* pp. 249ff.

[29] *Ibid.,* p. 236.

[30] *Ibidem.*

[31] *Ibid.,* pp. 254ff.

[32] *Ibid.,* pp. 251-254.

[33] *Ibid.,* p. 250.

[34] See Paul Guyer, *Kant,* Routledge, London, Special Indian Edn., 2006, p.68.

[35] H. E. Allison, *Kant's Transcendental Idealism : An Interpretation and Defense,* Yale University Press, New Haven, CT, revised edition, 2004, p. 35ff.

[36] H. E. Matthews, 'Strawson on 'Transcendental Idealism', in R.C.S. Walker, ed., *Kant on Pure Reason,* Oxford University Press, Oxford, 1982, pp. 132-149.

[37] Ralf Meerbote, 'The Unknowability of Things in Themselves', in Beck, ed., *Proceedings of the Third International Kant Congress,* 1972, pp. 415-423.

[38] For an overview of the literature, see Karl Ameriks, *Interpreting Kant's Critiques,* Clarendon, Oxford, 2003, pp. 69-78 (out of pp. 67-97).

[39] Guyer, *op. cit.,* pp. 67-68.

[40] Matthews' paper, in Walker, *op. cit.,* p. 136.

[41] *Critique,* Bxxvii.

[42] Cf. Allison, *op. cit.,* p. 56.

[43] Cf. Matthews' paper referred to.

[44] Strawson, *op. cit.,* p. 235; cf. his expression the 'phantasmagoric quality'.

[45] *Ibidem.*

[46] Matthews' paper, in Walker, *op. cit.,* p. 145.

[47] Strawson, *op. cit.,* p. 249 [already referred to in note 28 above].

[48] Matthews' paper, in Walker, *op. cit.,* p. 147.

[49] Strawson, *op. cit.,* p. 241.

[50] Matthews' paper, in Walker, *op. cit.* (2nd para.)

[51] On the notion of 'transcendental arguments', see particularly Barry Stroud, 'Transcendental Arguments', in *The Journal of Philosophy,* LXV, 1968, pp. 241-256, and see also R.C.S. Walker, *Kant: The Arguments of the Philosophers,* Routledge and Kegan Paul, London, 1978, pp. 10-13, 14-23.

[52] Cf. Gardner, 'Kant', in Grayling, *op. cit.,* p. 604.

[53] *Critique,* B275.

[54] Cf. Guyer, *op. cit.,* p. 122 (2nd para., lines 9-10).

[55] *Vide ibid.,* p. 121.

[56] *Ibid.,* p. 122.

[57] *Ibidem.*

[59] R. Schacht, *Classical Modern Philosophers : Descartes to Kant*, Routledge, London, 2003, p. 248.

[60] H. J. Paton, *Kant's Metaphysic of Experience*, Vol. One, George Allen & Unwin, London, 1970, Ch. LI, pp. 377f. Paton says : 'In the second edition the emphasis on empirical realism becomes much stronger, ...'

[61] *Critique*, Bxxxix, Kemp Smith's translation, p. 34, footnote.

CHAPTER SEVEN

MOORE'S PROOF OF AN EXTERNAL WORLD I (EXPLANATION OF SOME POINTS)

7.1 Foreword

In his well-known paper, 'Proof of an External World', G. E. Moore gives a proof of the existence of external things in the sense explicated in the paper. Towards the end of his paper, he observes :

> I can now give a large number of different proofs, each of which is a perfectly rigorous proof; and .... at many other times I have been in a position to give others.[1]

His 'large number of different proofs' are, however, 'essentially variations of the first proof he presents', as Avrum Stroll aptly points out.[2] Stroll, therefore, comments that it is Moore's first proof which is generally known as 'Moore's proof'. This comment is helpful, because it enables us to avoid the cumbrous locution 'Moore's proof or proofs'.

That, even after Kant, Moore should attempt a new proof of his own is apparently strange, considering the fact that Kant in the Preface to the second edition of his *Critique of Pure Reason* has claimed that the proof given by himself in that edition is a strict, and, as he believes, the only possible, proof.[3] There is, therefore, some need for explanation of the reason or reasons why Moore should give again a proof of his own. Of such a need Moore has shown himself to be aware in his paper, which, therefore, he begins by trying to explain why he, for one, thinks that Kant has not after all settled finally the problem of the existence of an external world.

After giving this explanation, however, Moore does not straightway attempt to prove the existence of external things. For he considers it very important at first to explicate the meaning of the expression 'external things'. For otherwise - as he thinks - it may not be clear what sort of things are the things the existence of which he is going to prove when he says that he will soon prove the existence of external things.

Moore's justification for writing his paper at all, and his explication there of the notion of external things, constitute the bulk of the paper, as occupying the first eighteen pages of (what Stroll has come to call) 'a twenty-three-page paper',[4] of which only the last five pages are devoted to the presentation of the proof proper, with Moore's meta-commentary on it.

The present chapter is concerned only with the preliminary, yet very important, matters treated of by Moore in that part of his paper which precedes his proof and his meta-remarks on it. His proof and his observations on it will be studied in the next chapter.

We may, then, begin this chapter by indicating Moore's objective in his paper under reference, and his plea for attempting a new proof of the existence of external things.

7.2 Moore's Objective in His Paper, 'Proof of an External World', and His Plea for Attempting Such a Proof

At the start of his paper, Moore quotes the following words from the Preface to the second edition of Kant's *Critique of Pure Reason* (in Kemp Smith's translation) :

> it still remains a scandal to philosophy .... that the existence of things outside of us .... must be accepted merely on *faith*, and that, if anyone thinks good to doubt

> their existence, we are unable to counter his doubts by any satisfactory proof.
>
> [Bxxxix, note : Kemp Smith, p. 34]

Moore in this connection observes :

> There seems to me to be no doubt whatever that it is a matter of some importance and also a matter which falls properly within the province of philosophy to discuss the question what sort of proof, if any, can be given of 'the existence of things outside of us.' And to discuss this question was my object when I began to write the present lecture.[5]

This observation does not, however, adequately express Moore's objective in the paper. For he says :

> But I may say at once that, as you will find, I have only, at most, succeeded in saying a very small part of what ought to be said about it.[6]

Moore's objective in his paper under consideration will become further clear in the light of what he has said in the later two paragraphs in the paper. ,

In the sentence immediately preceding the one quoted above from the second-edition Preface to the *Critique*, Kant claims, with regard to his proof in that edition, that this is 'a strict (also, as I believe, the only possible) proof of the objective reality of outer intuition [i.e. of the real existence of objects of outer intuition]'. This implies that he has removed a scandal to philosophy once for all by publishing a *satisfactory* proof of the existence of things outside of us. This involves, indeed, the tacit claim on the part of Kant that what it remains for any subsequent philosopher to do is only to repeat the proof which he (Kant) has provided, and to realize that the state of things which he has described has at last come to an end with the publication of his proof. It is this tacit claim on Kant's part which Moore, for himself, is unable to endorse. For he thinks that it is doubtful whether Kant's proof is satisfactory. Thus, he says :

> But I think it is by no means certain that Kant's proof is satisfactory. I think it is by no means certain that he did succeed in removing once for all the state of affairs which he considered to be a scandal to philosophy. And I think, therefore, that the question whether it is possible to give *any* satisfactory proof of the point in question still deserves discussion.[7]

Moore's plea for reopening the issue which Kant claims, at least tacitly, that he has finally settled, and also his (the former's) objective in his paper under consideration, will have been clear by now. His objective is to take up a challenge laid down by Kant, namely, to rid philosophy of a scandal by giving a proof of the existence of things outside of us in space.

7.3 Moore's Explication of the Phrase 'Things Outside of Us'

As his first step, Moore seeks to achieve full clarity as to the meaning of the expression 'things outside of us'; for, he thinks, everything else depends on this point.

The Kantian expression 'der Dinge ausser uns'[8] ('things outside of us') is rather odd, and its meaning is not quite clear. It might be replaced by the expression 'external things', which is less odd and of which the meaning can be made clearer by pointing out, as Moore says, 'that this phrase has been regularly used by philosophers as short for "things external to *our minds*".'[9] Philosophers generally use the three expressions 'external things', 'things external to *us*', and 'things external to *our minds*' as if they were perfectly synonymous and as if no explanation were needed. But Moore observes that of the three expressions the last is the clearest, 'since it at least makes clear that what is meant is not "external to *our bodies*",'[10] whereas each of the other two expressions as they stand is ambiguous between 'things external to our minds' and 'things external to our bodies'. But even the expression 'external to our minds' is not, for Moore, perfectly clear : if what is meant by 'proof of the existence of things outside of us' is to be made 'really clear', it will not do to say merely that 'outside of us' means 'external to our minds'.

7.3.1 Towards an elucidation of the meaning of the phrase 'external of our minds'

The phrase 'external to our minds' is not altogether free from ambiguity. Things in themselves in the philosophy of Kant are thought to be things which are external to our minds in so far as they are thought to exist apart from us (in Moore's translation, 'distinct from us')[11]; and Moore is not concerned with finding a proof of the existence of things in themselves. Kant distinguishes between two senses of 'external' : transcendental sense and empirical sense. Things in themselves are things which might be called external in the transcendental sense, while objects which are within the bounds of experience are *'empirically external* objects'. In order to make the latter concept quite unambiguous Kant distinguishes empirically external objects from those which may be said to be external in the transcendental sense, by explicitly calling the former 'things which are to be met with in space'.[12] [The German expression, which Kemp Smith translates as 'things which are to be found in space', is here translated by Moore as 'things which are to be met with in space'.]

7.3.1.1 Moore on the expression 'Things which are to be met with in space' : clarification of the sense in which he intends the word 'things' in this expression to be taken

Moore fixes upon the Kantian expression 'things which are to be met with in space', and observes that this 'does indicate fairly clearly what sort of things it is with regard to which I wish to inquire what sort of proof, if any, can be given that there are any things of that sort'.[13] All things of the sort that philosophers usually call 'physical objects', 'material things', or 'bodies' - such as my body, the bodies of other men, the bodies of animals, stones, mountains, the sun, the moon, chairs, tables, etc. - come under this head, according to him. Moore hastens to point out, however, that the phrase 'things which are to be met with in space' is naturally applicable in cases where the expression 'physical objects' or 'material things' or 'bodies' is hardly applicable. For example, shadows are not, properly speaking, physical objects or material things or bodies, and yet the phrase 'things which are to be met with in space' can well be applied to them, if this phrase is understood, as it can naturally be understood, in the wider neutral sense of 'whatever can be met with in space'.[14] Shadows are not things in the strong sense of 'bodies', but are still things in the neutral sense of 'items'; and such items are among those which are to be met with in space. Moore makes his intention clear by saying that he wishes to use the phrase 'things which are to be met with in space' in the wider sense of 'whatever can be met with in space'; and he avers that, if he does so, his purpose will still be served. His own words are here worth quoting :

> I wish the phrase 'things which are to be met with in space' to be understood in the wide sense; so that if a proof can be found that there ever have been as many as two different shadows it will follow at once that there have been at least two 'things which were to be met with in space', and this proof will be as good a proof of the point in question as would be a proof that there have been at least two 'physical objects' of no matter what sort.[15]

7.3.1.2 Moore's distinction between the expression 'to be met with in space' and the expression 'presented in space'

A comparison of the phrase 'things to be met with in space' with another phrase used by Kant is considered by Moore to be necessary for avoidance of confusions. At A373 of the *Critique,* Kant says that an 'empirical object' 'is called *external,* if it is presented *(vorgestellt) in space';* [quoted by Moore in his own translation.][16] Moore seeks to show that the phrase 'to be met with in space' and the phrase 'presented in space' are not equivalent.

Thus, he argues, examples can be given of'things', of which it can be allowed that they are 'presented in space', but of which it must be denied that they are 'to be met with in space'.

A negative after-image, or as it is also called, a negative after-sensation, is an example in point.[17] Moore quotes the following words from Foster :

> If, after looking steadfastly at a white patch on a black ground, the eye be turned to a white ground, a grey patch is seen for some little time. [Moore's reference : Foster, *Text-book of Physiology,* IV, iii, 3, p. 1266; quoted in Stout's *Manual of Psychology,* 3rd edn., p. 280][18]

After carrying out the experiment described here, by cutting out of a piece of white paper a four-pointed star, placing it on a black ground, then looking steadfastly at it, and thereafter turning his eyes to a white sheet of paper, Moore found that he saw a grey patch for some little time. He repeated the experiment 'successfully several times',[19] as he subsequently reports. Now a grey star 'seen' on a white background under the circumstances described is an after-image, and it is surely 'presented in space', he claims. But it is not, he contends, a thing 'to be met with in space'.[20] The white paper star originally looked at steadfastly, the black ground on which it is seen, and the white ground on which later the after-image is seen are no doubt all 'things to be met with in space' : they are indeed 'physical objects'[21] or surfaces of physical objects. But unlike any one of them, the after-image, which is 'presented in space', is not 'to be met with in space'. To say that the white paper star originally looked at steadfastly is a 'physical object' and is 'to be met with in space' is to imply that anyone else, who has normal eyesight, a normal sense of touch and is placed in *the same* circumstances, might have seen and felt it.[22] But it is not conceivable that anyone else should have seen the *same* grey after-image. Anyone else might have conceivably seen an after-image *very like* the one seen by the first man in question; but Moore says that

> there is an absurdity in supposing that . . . . 'two different people can ever see the *very same* after-image.'[23]

Thus a negative after-image is something which is 'presented in space', but is not a thing 'to be met with in space'. It is not, therefore, to be regarded as a thing which is 'external to our minds.'[24]

Moore has taken some other examples to illustrate his point in question.[25] Those other examples, however, add nothng substantially new, and may therefore be ignored.[26]

7.3.1.3 What is, for Moore, the true relation between 'external to our minds' and 'to be met with in space' ?

From the above discussion, the impression must not be had that the expressions 'external to our minds' and 'to be met with in space' are, for Moore, synonymous. He clearly says : ' "external to our minds" is not a mere synonym for "to be met with in space" : that is to say, "external to our minds" and "to be met with in space" are two different conceptions'.[27] This needs some explanation :

Since the term *'our* minds' means the minds of human beings, it follows, as Moore argues, that any pains which animals may feel, any experiences they may have, cannot be *in* our minds, but must be external to *our minds.* Yet it is not to be allowed that these things or items - namely, pains felt by animals, or experiences had by them - are, for that matter, things or items to be met with in space.[28] Hence, being *external to our minds* and being *things to be met with in space* are two different conceptions, according to Moore. That is to say, the terms 'external to our minds' and 'to be met with in space' are not, for him, synonymous.

The true relation, for Moore, between 'external to our minds' and 'to be met with in space' may now be stated as follows :

If any things be such that they are to be met with in space, then they are external things, that is, (empirical) things external to our minds; but the converse may not be true : for example, pains presumably felt by animals are things (items) external to *our minds,* but are not things to be met with in space.

This chapter may be brought to a close by quoting the following words from Moore's paper under consideration :

> We have already seen that there are ever so many kinds of 'things', such that, in the case of each of these kinds, from the proposition that there is at least one thing of that kind there *follows* the proposition that there is at least one thing to be met with in space : e.g., this follows from 'There is at least one star', from 'There is at least one human body', from 'There is at least one shadow', etc. And I think we can say that of every kind of thing of which this is true, it is also true that from the proposition that there is at least one 'thing' of that kind there *follows* the proposition that there is at least one thing external to our minds : e.g., from 'There is

> at least one star' there follows not only 'There is at least one thing to be met with in space' but also 'There is at least one external thing', and similarly in all other cases.[29]

In the next chapter it will be seen how Moore presents his proof or proofs of the existence of the sort of things in question.

NOTES

1 Moore, 'Proof of an External World', reprinted (from *Proceedings of the British Academy,* Vol. XXV, 1939, pp. 273-300) in R. R. Ammerman, ed., *Classics of Analytic Philosophy,* Tata McGraw-Hill, Bombay, 1965, p. 81; also reprinted (from Moore, *Philosophical Papers,* George Allen & Unwin, London, 1959) in L. P. Pojman, ed., *Classics of Philosophy,* Oxford University Press, Oxford, 1998, p. 1144 (out of pp. 1141-1146).

2 See Avrum Stroll, *Moore and Wittgenstein on Certainty,* Oxford University Press, Oxford, 1994, p. 55.

3 *Critique,* Bxxxix.

4 Stroll, *op. cit.,* p. 58.

5 Moore's paper, in Ammerman, p. 69, and in Pojman, p. 1142.

6 *Ibidem;* Ammerman, *loc. cit.*

7 *Ibid.* p. 70; Pojman, *loc. cit.*

8 Kant, *Kritik der reinen Vernunft* (1787), ed., Theodor Valentiner, FELIX MEINER, LEIPZIG, 1922, p. 42.

9 Pojman, *op. cit.,* p. 1142. Ammerman, p. 70.

10 *Ibibem.*

11 *Ibidem.*

12 *Ibidem.*

13 *Ibidem,* (last para.)

14 *Ibid.,* p. 71.

15 *Ibidem.*

16 *Ibidem* (3rd para.)

17 *Ibidem.*

18 *Ibidem.*

19 *Ibidem* (last line of the last para.)

20 *Ibid.,* p. 72.

21 *Ibidem.*

[22] *Ibidem.*

[23] *Ibidem.*

[24] *Ibidem.* (2nd para.)

[25] *Ibid.*, pp. 72-74.

[26] For a lucid and comprehensive expository account of Moore's distinction between 'presented in space' and 'to be met with in space; see E.D. Klemke, *The Epistemology of G. E. Moore,* Northwestern University Press, Evanston, 1969, esp. pp. 144-146.

[27] Pojman, *op. cit.*, p. 1143. See Ammerman, p. 80.

[28] *Ibidem.* Pojman, *loc. cit.*

[29] *Ibidem.* Ammerman, p. 80.

CHAPTER EIGHT

MOORE'S PROOF OF AN EXTERNAL WORLD II (EXPLANATION OF SOME OTHER POINTS)

8.1 Foreword

In his paper 'Proof of an External World' Moore has presented two proofs concerning the existence of external things. What he means by 'external things' has already been explained by himself in the proof-preceding part of his paper, as has been taken note of in the last chapter.[1] The qualifications, refinements, etc., introduced by him in order to make his conception of external things adequately clear are important, in that his proofs, which are excessively brief, can hardly be appreciated as being proofs of *external things* except through his preceding clarifications. In this respect, there is some importance in Klemke's observation that, in each case of the proofs presented by Moore, what he (Moore) calls the proof is only one stage in a larger complex proof developed through his paper.[2]

With reference to each of his proofs, Moore claims that he can,[3] or could,[4] give a large number of different proofs, each of which is a rigorous proof, of the existence of things outside of us. Since such a claim has been left at a purely assertoric level by him, we have only followed the usual practice of Moore-interpreters in setting it aside.

As regards each of the two proofs actually presented by him, Moore claims, again, that it is a rigorous proof. This is a claim which he has tried his best to substantiate indeed. He lays down the conditions necessary for a rigorous proof, and then seeks, in the case of each of the two proofs, to show that it satisfies those conditions.

In the last two paragraphs of his paper he points out the reasons why 'many philosophers'[5] (at times he says, 'some people')[6] would, he thinks, still feel dissatisfied with his proofs, and tries to show that those reasons are not sound.

As is found, Moore is here talking in terms of his *two* proofs (which he calls 'my two proofs').[7] We, however, generally talk of 'Moore's proof' (in the singular), and mean thereby his first proof. There is a sense in which indeed his first proof is the more fundamental, because - as will be transparent later on - his second proof is essentially a variation of his first proof. This is a point which is only mentioned here in order to set our records straight.

In the present chapter Moore's two proofs are stated first, and then his claims and observations on them come also to be studied. The account presented here is merely expository and interpretative. A critical examination of his 'proof of an external world' is undertaken in the ninth chapter.

8.2 Moore's 'Two Proofs' Stated, and Explained Briefly

The presentation of Moore's first proof along with the necessary explanations follows.

8.2.1 Presentation, with explanation, of the first proof

Moore says :

> I can prove now, for instance, that two human hands exist. How ? By holding up my two hands and saying, as I make a gesture with the right, 'Here is one hand', and adding, as I make a certain gesture with the left, 'and here is another'. And if, by doing this, I have proved *ipso facto* the existence of external things, you will all see that

> I can also do it now in numbers of other ways : there is no need to multiply examples.[8]

In the light of Moore's own explanation as contained in the above extract, his proof in question can be cast formally into the form of the following argument :

1) Here is one hand.
2) Here is another (hand).
3) Therefore two human hands exist.
4) Therefore some external things exist.

The transition from (3) to (4) should be, according to Moore, obvious in the light of the explanation given in the proof-preceding part of his paper. The hands shown by him satisfy the description of external things. They are things to be met with in space. They are not only seen by all persons on the audience at the same time; they can be also touched by anyone of them, if only he chooses to come and touch them. He will then be convinced that they are real hands and that they are external things which exist.

The logical character of Moore's argument can now be made further clear.

8.2.1.1 On the logical character of Moore's argument (proof) (in terms of Alice Ambrose's interpretation)

Let us, to start with, symbolize steps (1) to (3) in Moore's argument or proof :

$$Ha$$

$$Hb$$

$$\therefore (\exists x)\, Hx$$

> Strictly speaking, the conclusion follows from *either* prcmisc by EG.

Alice Ambrose puts the point as follows :

> The proof consists in proceeding from the assertedly known premise, 'Here is a hand', to the conclusion which logically follows from it, 'there exists a thing external to us'. It is analogous to a very common form of argument, viz., to that in which an existential assertion is established by pointing out a specific instance. One proves that there is an officer of the law in a given village by pointing out the local sheriff, that there is a coin in the collection plate by pointing out a penny. 'That (pointing) is a sheriff of village K' entails 'There is an officer of the law in village K' and 'there (pointing) is a penny in the collection plate' entails 'There is a coin . . .'. In the same way Moore points out a hand (i.e., a physical object, i.e., as he explains, an object to be met with in space), and from this it follows that there is an external object. 'Here (pointing) is a hand' entails 'There exists a hand', which entails 'There exists an external object.'[9]

It is time now to pass on to Moore's second proof.

8.2.2 Presentation, with some explanation, of Moore's second proof

Moore's second proof is concerned with proving 'that external objects have existed *in the past, ...*'[10]

As for his first proof, it proves only that external objects exist *now*. Because a man is waving his hands, it follows only that the hands he is referring to exist now. Therefore, the (first) conclusion in Moore's first proof, namely, step (3) - 'Therefore two human hands exist' - allows of being amplified so as to read : 'Therefore two human hands exist at this moment'.[11]

If, however, what Moore is asked to do is to prove that some external objects existed *in the past,* then he says : 'I can give many different proofs of this also, but proofs which are in important respects of a different sort. . . . .'[12] Then he gives one such proof :

> I can say : 'I held up two hands above this desk not very long ago; two hands existed not very long ago; therefore . . . . two external objects have existed at some time in the past, Q.E.D.'[13]

Moore is going to show next that the two proofs he has presented are 'rigorous'[14] ('conclusive',[15] 'satisfactory'[16]) proofs.

8.3 Whether or Not Moore's Two Proofs Are Rigorous, Satisfactory, Proofs (Determination, alongwith Necessary Explanation, of Moore's Own View in This Regard)

Moore has laid down three conditions necessary for a 'rigorous' ('satisfactory') proof.

8.3.1 The conditions necessary for a rigorous (satisfactory) proof, according to Moore

In his paper under consideration the expressions 'rigorous proof' and 'satisfactory proof' are used by Moore in the same sense. Now, the three conditions as required by him[17] in this regard may be stated as :

1) The premise by which the conclusion is proved must be different from the conclusion.
2) The premise must be one which is *known* to be true.
3) The conclusion must really follow from the premise.

For Moore, each of the three conditions is necessary for a rigorous proof.

8.3.2 Moore's own assessment of his first proof

Moore seeks to show now that his first proof satisfies the three conditions of a rigorous proof.

1) The premise 'here is one hand' differs from the conclusion 'Two human hands exist at this moment'. Moore argues that the premise and the conslusion are different, because the conclusion might have been true even if the premise had been false.[18]

2) Moore claims that he did at the moment *know* that the premise was true.

Moore is very certain that his premise in question is true. This means that there are no propositions which are *more certain* than his premise. This is to say that there is (or, are) no more fundamental proposition (or, propositions) which is (or are) *immediately* known to be true, such that from it (or, them) his premise can be logically deduced. It is his claim that his premise, and only a proposition like it, is to be counted among the very fundamental propositions, which implies that it is *known* to be true, and *immediately* known to be true.[19]

3) Moore says that 'it is quite certain' that the conclusion did follow from the premise. 'This is as certain as it is that if there is one hand here and another here *now*, then it follows that there are two hands in existence *now*'.[20]

Moore is thus convinced that his first proof satisfied all the three conditions for a rigorous proof.

8.3.3 Moore's own assessment of his second proof

With regard to his second proof, Moore holds that this also is a good and satisfactory proof, provided he *knows* what is asserted in its premise. But does he *know* what is asserted in the premise of his second proof to be true ? He answers in the affirmative, and he argues as follows :

> I *do* know that I held up two hands above this desk not very long ago. As a matter of fact, in this case you all know it too. There's no doubt whatever that I did.

> Therefore I have given a perfectly conclusive proof that external objects have existed in the past; . . . .[21]

From the above, Moore arrives at the conclusion : 'I have, then, given two conclusive proofs of the existence of external objects.'[22]

8.4 Moore's Answers to Some Anticipated Objections to His 'Two Proofs'

Moore anticipates that many philosophers will still feel that he has not given any satisfactory proof. One reason for this lingering feeling of dissatisfaction might be that Moore has not proved the propositions which he used as premises in his two proofs. The philosophers in question really want not only a proof of the premises in the two proofs in question, but also something like a general statement as to how any propositions of this sort may be proved.[22]

Moore in reply points out that he has not indeed given any proof of the premises themselves, and does not believe that this can be done. He says that in order to do it, he should need to prove, as Descartes pointed out, that he is not dreaming. He asks, 'How can I prove that I am not ?' He adds :

> I have, no doubt, conclusive reasons for asserting that I am not now dreaming; I have conclusive evidence that Iam awake : but that is a very different thing from being able to prove it. I could not tell you what all my evidence is; and I should require to do this at least, in order to give you a proof.[23]

Another, connected, objection anticipated by Moore is this. Thus, the dissatisfied philosophers would say : 'If you cannot prove your premise that here is one hand and here is another, then you do not know it. But you yourself have admitted that, if you did not know it, then your proof was not conclusive.

Therefore your proof was not, as you say it was, a conclusive proof.'[24]

In reply, Moore contends that the objection in question is based on a definitely mistaken assumption. The assumption is 'very common among philosophers' that if I cannot *prove* a proposition, then I cannot *know* it. This is a wrong assumption, according to Moore, who holds the view : 'I can know things, which I cannot prove'.[25] Moore has given a clear and strong argument in his book *Some Main Problems of Philosophy* to enforce this point. In this book he has argued that, if an *infinite regress* is to be avoided, we must hold that we can *know* many propositions to be true, even though we cannot *prove* them. To prove a proposition is to establish it as a conclusion from another proposition or set of propositions. But in order to prove the premises themselves, we must similarly deduce them from still other propositions, which again must be deducible from still further propositions, and so on *ad infinitum*. 'And it is quite certain that no man ever has thus known a really infinite series of propositions.' This argument constitutes a *reductio ad absurdum* of the view that to know any proposition to be true is to be able to prove it.[26]

That is why Moore in his paper 'Proof of an External World' holds : 'I can know things, which I cannot prove'. In this way he has answered the objection, under examination, to his two proofs of the existence of external things.

Although Moore has claimed that his 'proof of an external world' is satisfactory, we have to examine, however, whether his claim is ultimately tenable. This we do in the next chapter.

NOTES

1 See esp. 7.3 above.

2 E. D. Klemke, *The Epistemology of G. E. Moore,* Evanston, 1969, p. 147 n. 18.

3 See Moore's 'Proof of an External World' in R. R. Ammerman, ed., *Classics of Analytic Philosophy,* 1965, p. 81.

4 *Ibid.,* p. 83.

5 *Ibidem.*

6 *Ibid, p. 84.*

7 *Ibidem.*

8 *Ibid.,* p. 81

9 Alicc Ambrose, 'Moore's "Proof of an External World",' in *The Philosophy of G. E. Moore,* ed. P. A. Schilpp, The Library of Living Philosophers, New York, 2nd edn., 1952.

10 Ammerman; (ed.), *op. cit.,* p. 83.

11 Cf. *ibid.,* p. 82.

12 *Ibid.,* p. 83.

13 *Ibidem.*

14 *Ibid.,* p. 82.

15 *Ibid.,* p. 83.

16 *Ibidem.*

17 *Ibid.,* p. 82.

18 *Ibidem.*

19 For Moore's concept of *immediate knowledge* (as distinguished from direct apprehension), see his *Some Main Problems of Philosophy,* George Allen & Unwin, London, 1965, pp. 123f.

20 In Ammerman, p. 82.

21 *Ibid.,* p. 83.

22 Cf. *ibid.* p. 84.

23 *Ibidem.*

24 *Ibidem.*

25 *Ibidem.*

26 Cf. Moore's *Some Main Problems of Philosophy,* pp. 120-121.

CHAPTER NINE

AN EXAMINATION OF MOORE'S PROOF

9.1 Foreword

It has been seen that Moore in his paper 'Proof of an External World' has actually presented two proofs of the existence of external things in spacc. Of these two proofs, the first is the more fundamental, because his second proof, even though it is different in important respects from the first, is in a way essentially a variation of his first proof. It is, therefore, understandable why critics of Moore have chosen to consider his first proof only in assessing his proof of an external world.

As Moore's proof is the climax of his paper, it is only too natural that it is this which should be in the centre of our attention in this chapter. Only by concentrating on the proof, we may hope to be in a position to determine whether or not the proof has been ultimately successful in meeting the challenge made by a philosophical sceptic.

9.2 The Wittgensteinian Criticism of Moore's Proof Considered

Moore's proof has been criticized by Wittgenstein in his work *On Certainty.*[1] He inquires whether Moore's proof has been the right sort of proof for doing the right sort of job.

A proof of the sort which Moore has given can only be significant if it can allay the kind of doubts which some philosophers have expressed regarding the existence of the external world. More precisely, the question is whether Moore's proof sets at rest the kind of doubts which philosophical sceptics or some idealists raise as to the existence of external physical objects. Wittgenstein writes :

> 'Doubting the existence of the external world' does not mean, for example, doubting the existence of a planet, which later observations proved to exist, - or does Moore want to say that knowing that here is his hand is different from knowing the existence of the planet Saturn ? Otherwise it would be possible to point out the discovery of the planet Saturn to the doubters and say that its existence has been proved, and hence the existence of the external world as well.[2]

The above comment made by Wittgenstein involves the following sort of criticism of Moore.[3]

The philosophical sceptic's question about the existence of the external world is not like the question about the existence of Saturn. The latter question is a factual question such that it is decidable by the adducing of factual evidence. At one time there was some doubt whether a planet existed in a certain portion of space-time. Appropriate astronomical observations established that one did, and this planet was later named 'Saturn'. Since the doubt in this case was a genuine factual doubt, it allowed of being factually resolved : it *was* resolved by the adducing of factual evidence. But the philosophical-sceptic's doubt as to the existence of an external, physical, object is not at all a factual question which can be factually decided by the adducing of evidence. It is indeed a philosophical question, a non-factual issue, which cannot be resolved by the production of evidence. Moore's proof is designed to decide a non-factual issue by the production of factual evidence : taking his hand to be a specific instance of an external physical object, he tries to establish its existence by adducing evidence, namely, by raising and waving it. But was there ever any time after Moore was born that men, including Moore himself, doubted if Moore's hand exists ? Indeed, there never was any time, after his birth, when anyone doubted that his hand exists : from that time (the time after he was born) his hand was visible to anyone who at all cared to look at it. There was some doubt at one time whether a planet (Saturn) existed, and so, understandably, it was a factual doubt which could be, and in fact was, resolved by the production of factual (here, astronomical) evidence. There was no analogous doubt, entertained by anyone, about the existence of Moore's hand, and so it was quite irrelevant on Moore's part to have sought to prove its existence by the production of factual evidence.

Thus, Wittgenstein's criticism comes to this, that Moore's proof was misdirected : it misses the philosophical-sceptic's point. He fails to see that the issue raised by a philosophical-sceptic is a philosophical issue, and not a factual issue. As a result, he has failed to meet the challenge laid down by a sceptic. He has done the irrelevant sort of thing by trying to resolve philosophical (i.e. non-factual) doubts through the factual means by the adducing of evidence.

We have come to a point at which it will be relevant and effective to consider Don Locke's criticism of Moore's Proof.

9.3 Consideration of Don Locke's Criticism of Moore's Proof

Moore's Proof is usually stated in three steps.[4] But those three steps do not express his line of thinking adequately. He means to prove that external things exist, but has only proved that human hands exist. Clearly, he has not expressed all the steps which are needed to serve his purpose. He thinks that his readers will be able to supply the requisite steps by themselves in the light of his whole discussion, and in keeping with his intention, in his paper under reference.

Accordingly, Don Locke restates Moore's proof as follows in the light of Moore's whole discussion, and in keeping with his intention, in his paper under reference :

1) 1 am holding up a human hand.
2) Human hands are physical objects.
3) Physical objects are external objects.
4) Therefore I am holding up an external object.
5) Therefore, an external object exists.[5]

> [A student of logic may appreciate that, in order that the conclusion may follow, it will do to state the first premise by reference to a single hand.]

According to Moore, the premises in a good argument must be true and known to be true. So the above argument cannot be a good argument, unless its premises are true and known to be true. But are the premises really such ?

It seems to be natural to hold that steps (2) and (3) in Moore's proof are analytic, and that (1) is, in some sense to be considered later, obvious and unquestionable.[6]

Let us consider the third premise of the above argument, namely, step (3) : 'Physical objects are external objects'. According to Moore, the proposition is *obviously true.* This suggests that it is analytic, that is, true by definition.

But if the proposition - that physical objects are external objects - is analytic - i.e. true by definition - , then it is necessarily true. On Moore's view, the proposition is, then, necessarily true, i.e. unquestionably true. Yet an Idealist like Berkeley would, surely, question the truth of this proposition. And he would question it without any self-contradiction on his part. Let us try to be a bit more clear.

The proposition, 'physical objects are external objects', is analytic if and only if the term 'physical object' has its ordinary

Realist sense. But it is open to an Idealist to give the term some other sense in which it is not true - and so not necessarily true - that physical objects are external objects. For example, Berkeley was prepared to talk about physical objects, but not to talk about external objects, from which it follows that what he meant by the expression 'physical object' was not precisely what we ordinarily mean by it.[7]

To come now to the first step in the argument under consideration : Two ways of supporting it are open to Moore—

One way of supporting it is by means of the paradigm case argument, by saying that this is a paradigm example of a human hand. That is, it cannot be denied that this is a human hand, because to deny this would be to cut this expression off from the very cases from which it obtains its meaning. If this is not a human hand, what can be ? Against this, Don Locke argues as follows :

> It is indeed true that in one way 'hand' is such a word, because to be a hand is to possess 'certain observable and ostensively indicable features', but the conclusion cannot follow unless it is shown that it is a hand in a stronger sense - in the sense that it can exist even when it is not perceived. But that it can exist even when it is not perceived cannot be shown by reference to its observable and ostensively indicable features. So the paradigm case argument cannot establish that it is a hand in this stronger sense.[8]

The other way of supporting the first step in Moore's proof is to argue that the proposition cannot be shown to be false, because it is more certain than the premises of any argument which may be given to show that it is false. Don Locke here comments as follows :

> Now certainly no philosopher has ever been so rash as

> to deny that this sort of thing is a hand, but, as Moore himself allows, they can disagree about what human hands are. The question is not so much whether it is undeniable that this is a hand as whether it is undeniable that this, a hand, is a physical object in the ordinary Realist sense. This, clearly, is not undeniable, and to insist that it is, is really nothing more than a refusal to argue the point at issue between Realist and Idealist. So although it is undeniable that this is, in some sense, a hand, it is not undeniable in any sense from which it follows that this object exists unperceived. And what is in dispute is not whether human hands exist but whether they really exist, whether they are objects that continue to exist unperceived.[9]

In fine, the Idealist, and a philosopher of an idealistic-sceptical persuasion, have Moore in a dilemma : Either the first premise in his proof is not strong enough for the third premise to follow, or, if it is strong enough, its truth cannot be established in the way he seeks to establish it.[10] Moore in his proof under consideration has either failed to see, or simply refused to argue, the point at issue between Realist and Idealist. His proof has not been, after all, successful.

To conclude : Moore's proof of an external world has been found, on an examination, to be such that we are unable to say that we accept it.

It remains to add a concluding note on this work as a whole hereinafter.

NOTES

[1] Ludwing Wittgenstein, *On Certainty,* trans. Denis Paul and G. E. M. Anscombe, ed. Anscombe and G. H. von Wright, Harper Torchbooks, Harper and Row, New York, 1972.

[2] *Ibid.,* 20, p. 4e.

[3] For interpretation of Wittgenstein's criticism, see Avrum Stroll, *Moore and Wittgenstein on Certainty,* Oxford University Press, Oxford, 1994, pp. 101ff.

[4] *Ibidem,* p. 56.

[5] Don Locke, *Perception and Our Knowledge of the External World,* George Allen & Unwin, London, 1967, pp. 129-130.

[6] *Ibid.,* p. 130.

[7] *Ibidem.*

[8] *Ibid.,* pp. 130-131.

[9] *Ibid.,* p. 131.

[10] *Ibidem.*

CONCLUDING NOTE ON THIS WORK AS A WHOLE

The proofs of the existence of external things in space as given by Descartes, Kant, and Moore, have all of them been interpreted in the present work with full attention to the various interpretative issues raised by them, and all of them have been examined in detail with equally full attention to the various pertinent critical issues they give rise to. It has been found that, unlike Descartes' and Moore's proofs, the two proofs presented by Kant in the two editions of the *Critique of Pure Reason* are eminently susceptible of defence against objections.

Hence we come to think that, even if Descartes' and Moore's proofs are, contrary to their own opinions, unsatisfactory, the Kantian proofs are, in their own ways, tolerably satisfactory. Kant's second-edition proof, however, has, as we have argued in 6.4, a better title to acceptance.

Kant regards Descartes' proof as unsatisfactory, and has given reasons why he so regards it. Moore in his turn thinks that Kant's second-edition proof - which alone, indeed, he (Moore) has considered - is not, even though Kant himself claims it to be, a satisfactory proof. But although Moore has said that he thinks it is not certain that Kant's proof is satisfactory, he does not explain, however, why he thinks so. Moore has left, then, his anti-Kantian comment at a purely assertoric level. It is not certain, therefore, that Moore's comment is not dogmatic.

So, pending further research, we may conclude this work by saying that, of the three philosophers' proofs of the existence of external things in space, as considered in the present work, the proof given by Kant, especially in the second-edition of the *Critique*, has the best title to our acceptance.

BIBLIOGRAPHY

Alexander, P., *Ideas, Qualities and Corpuscles,* Cambridge University Press, Cambridge, 1985.

Allison, H. E., *Kant's Transcendental Idealism : An Interpretation and Defense,* Yale University Press, New Haven, CT, revised edition, 2004.

Ambrose, Alice, 'Moore's "Proof of an External World" ', in P. A., Schilpp, (ed.) *The Philosophy of G. E. Moore* (see below).

Ameriks, K., *Interpreting Kant's Critiques,* Clarendon, Oxford, 2003.

Arnauld, Antoine, *On True and False Ideas,* trans. E. J. Kremer, Edwin Mellen Press, Lampeter, 1990, pp. 176ff.

Aquila, R., 'Concepts, Objects and the Analytic in Kant', in L. W. Beck., (ed.) *Proceedings of the Third International Kant Congress,* (1970), (see below)

Beck, L. W., (ed.) *Proceedings of the Third International Kant Congress,* (1970), D. Reidel, Dordrecht - Holland, 1972.

Bennett, J., *Learning from Six Philosophers : Descartes, Spinoza, Leibniz, Locke, Berkeley, Hume,* Vol 2, Clarendon, Oxford, First published 2001, in paperback 2003.

Bennett, J., *Kant's Analytic,* Cambridge University Press, Cambridge, 1966.

Berkeley, G., *Treatise Concerning the Principles of Human Knowledge* (1710), in A. C. Fraser, (ed.) *Selections from Berkeley,* Annotated, (see below).

Berkeley, G., *'A New Theory of Vision', Selections from Berkeley,* Annotated, A. C. Fraser, (see below)

Bird, Graham, *Kant's Theory of Knowledge,* Routledge & Kegan Paul, London, 1962, 2nd impression, 1965.

Bracken, Harry M., *Descartes,* Oneworld Publications, Oxford, First South Asian Edition, 2007, p. 92.

Brittan, Jr., G. G., *Kant's Theory of Science,* Princeton University Press, Princeton, New Jersey, 1978.

Broad, C. D., *Kant : An Introduction,* ed. C. Lewy, Cambridge University Press, Cambridge, reprinted, 1979.

Burnham, D., and Young H., 'Kant's *Critique of Pure Reason',* Edinburgh University Press, Edinburgh, 2007, pp. 127f.

Burnyeat, M. F., 'Idealism and Greek Philosophy : What Descartes Saw and Berkeley Missed', in *Philosophical Review* 91, 1982, pp. 3-40.

Copleston, S. J., *A History of Philosophy,* Vol. VI *{Modern Philosophy : from The French Enlightenment to Kant),* Doubleday, New York, Image ed. 1994.

Cottingham, J., 'Descartes' *Sixth Meditation* : The External World, "Nature" and Human Experience', in G. Vesey (ed.), *Philosophers : Ancient and Modern,* Cambridge University Press, London, 1986.

Cottingham, J. C, *Descartes,* Basil Blackwell, Oxford, 1986.

Curley, E. M., *Descartes against the Sceptics,* Blackwell, Oxford, 1978.

Descartes, R., *Meditations on the First Philosophy,* trans. John Veitch, Everyman's Library, Dent, London, last reprinted, 1949. Also in *Ten Great Works of Philosophy,* Robert Paul Wolff (ed.), Mentor, Penguin Books, USA Inc, New York, 1969.

Descartes, R., *The Prinicíples of Philosophy,* trans. J. Veitch, Everyman's Library, Dent, London, last reprinted, 1949.

Descartes, R., *A Discourse on Method,* trans, and ed., J. Veitch, Dent, London, 1949.

Descartes, R., *Conversation with Burman,* trans, and ed., J. Cottingham, Clarendon, Oxford, 1976.

Descartes, R., *The Philosophical Writings of Descartes,* trans, and edited by J. Cottingham, R. Stoothoff, and D. Murdoch, Cambridge University Press, 1984-85.

Ewing, A. C., *A Short Commentary on Kant's Critique of Pure REASON,* Methuen & Co. Ltd., London, 1961.

Falckenberg, R., *History of Philosophy,* trans. A. C. Armstrong, Jr., Progressive Publishers, Calcutta, 1962.

Fraser, A. C, *Selections from Berkeley,* Annotated, Clarendon, Oxford, 1910.

Gardner, S., 'Kant' in A. C. Grayling (ed.), *Philosophy 2,* Oxford University Press, Oxford, reprinted in paperback 2007.

Garve, C, First review of the *Critique* in the *Göttingen Journal*, January 19, 1782; see for trans. B. Sassen (ed.), *Kańt's Early Critics : The Empiricist Critique of the Theoretical Philosophy*, Cambridge University Press, Cambridge, 2000.

Gibson, A. Boyce, *The Philosophy of Descartes*, Methuen, London, 1932.

Gilson, E., *Etudes sur le ròle de la pensée médiévale dans la formation du systéme cartésiene*, J. Vrim, Paris, 1951, extracts trans. A. K. Stout in 'Descartes' Proof of the Existence of Matter', *Philosophy* (see below).

Groarke, L., Descartes' *First Meditation* : Something Old, Something New, Something Borrowed' in *Journal of the History of Philosophy 22*, 1984, pp. 281-301.

Guyer, Paul, *The Cambridge Companion to Kant*, Cambridge University Press, Cambridge, reprinted 1999. ,

Guyer, Paul, *Kant*, Routledge, Taylor & Francis Group, First published 2006, First Indian Reprint 2008.

Kant, I., *Kritik der reinen Vernunft* (1787), (ed.) Theodor Valentiner, Felix Meiner, Leipzig, 1922.

Kant, I., *Prolegomena to Any Future Metaphysics*, trans, and ed. L. W. Beck, Library of Liberal Arts, Bobbs - Merrill Co. Inc, Indianapolis, 1976.

Kant, I., *Critique of Pure Reason*, First Edition 1781, Second Edition, 1787, trans. Norman Kemp Smith, Macmillan, London, 1968. For translation of some portions of the *Critique*, see also Mahaffy and Bernard (see below).

Keeling, S. V., *Descartes,* Second edition, Oxford University Press, London, 1968.

Klemke, E. D., *The Epistemology of G. E. Moore,* Northwestern University Press, Evanston, 1969.

Locke, Don, *Perception and Our Knowledge of the External World,* George Allen & Unwin, London, 1967; Ch. 8.2 ('Moore's Proof of an External World'), pp. 129-131.

Locke, John, *An Essay Concerning Human Understanding,* abridged and ed. by John W. Yolton, Everyman's Library, reprinted, 1992.

Mahaffy, J. P. and Bernard J. H., *Kant's Critical Philosophy,* Orient Publications, Delhi, First Indian Reprint 1988.

Matthews, H. E., 'Strawson on Transcendental Idealism', in R. C. S. Walker, (ed.), *Kant on Pure Reason,* pp. 132-49. (see below).

McCracken, C. J., and Tipton, S. C, (eds.) *Berkeley's Principles and Dialogues : Background Source Materials,* Cambridge University Press, Cambridge, U.K., 2000, p. 8 n.l.

Meerbote, R., 'The Unknowability of Things in Themselves', in Beck, (ed.) *Proceedings of the Third International Kant Congress,* 1972, pp. 415-423. (see above).

Moore, G. E., 'Proof of an External World', reprinted (from *Proceedings* of the British Academy, Vol. XXV, 1939) in R. R. Ammerman, (ed.), *Classics of Analytic Philosophy,* pp. 273-300. Also reprinted (from Moore, *Philosophical Papers,* George Allen & Unwin, London, 1959) in L. P. Pojman., *(ed.) Classics of Philosophy,* pp. 1141-1146.

Moore, G. E., *Some Main Problems of Philosophy,* George Allen & Unwin, London, 1965, pp. 123f.

Parsons, C, 'The Transcendental Aesthetic', in Paul Guyer (ed.), *The Cambridge Companion to Kant* (see above), pp. 62-100.

Paton, H. J., *Kant's Metaphysic of Experience,* Volumes One and Two, George Allen & Unwin, London, 1970.

Prichard, H. A., *Kant's Theory of Knowledge,* Clarendon, Oxford, 1909.

Reschcr, N., *The Primacy of Practice,* Basil Blackwell, Oxford, 1973.

Russell, B., *Our Knowledge of the External World,* Open Court, London, 1914.

Schacht, R., *Classical Modern Philosophers : Descartes to Kant,* Routledge, London, transferred to Digital Printing 2003.

Schlipp, P. A., (ed.) *The Philosophy of G. E. Moore,* The Library of Living Philosophers, New York, 2nd edn, 1952.

Smith, N. K., *New Studies in the Philosophy of Descartes,* Macmillan, London, 1952.

Smith, N. K., *A Commentary to Kant's 'Critique of Pure Reason',* Macmillan & Co., Ltd, London, 1918.

Stoothoff. R., 'Descartes' Dilemma', in *The Philosophical Quarterly,* Vol. 39, No. 156, July 1989, Basil Blackwell, pp. 294-307.

Stout, A. K., 'Descartes' Proof of the Existence of Matter', *Philosophy,* International Philosophical Quarterly, Vol. 1, 1961, New York, 1961, pp. 191-207.

Strawson, P. F., *The Bounds of Sense,* Methuen, London, 1966.

Stroll, A., *Moore and Wittgenstein on Certainty,* Oxford University Press, Oxford, 1994.

Stroud, B., 'Transcendental Arguments', *The Journal of Philosophy,* LXV, 1968, pp. 241-256, also in R. C. S. Walker., (ed.) *Kant : The Arguments of The Philosophers* (see below).

Walker, R. C. S., (ed.) *Kant on Pure Reason,* Oxford University Press, Oxford, 1982.

Walker, R. C. S., *Kant: The Arguments of the Philosophers,* Routledge and Kegan Paul, London, 1978, pp. 10-13, 14-23.

Williams, B., *Descartes : The Project of Pure Enquiry,* Humanities Press, New Jersey, 1978.

Wilson, Margaret Dauler, *Descartes,* Routledge & Kegan Paul, London, 1978.

Wittgenstein, L., *On Certainty,* trans. Denis Paul and G. E. M. Anscombe, ed. Anscombe and G. H. von Wright, Harper Torchbooks, Harper and Row, New York, 1972.

index